Great Western Castle Class 4-6-0 Locomotives in the Preservation Era

Front cover photo: 5043 *Earl of Mount Edgcumbe* sprints along the sea wall in this classic view of the approach to Dawlish station with the return *Cornishman* railtour, 28 April, 2012. (Robin Coombes)

Back cover photos:
4073 *Caerphilly* Castle as restored in 1960 and now housed in STEAM Museum at Swindon. (STEAM Museum)

5029 *Nunney* Castle at Didcot Great Western Centre, May 2010. (David Maidment)

4079 *Pendennis* Castle at Didcot Great Western Centre after its restoration, launched on the weekend of 2-3 April 2022. (Adrian Knowles)

Inside back jacket: 7029 *Clun Castle*, after the hiatus in 2018, pauses on its first test run at Whitlocks End, 19 February 2019. (Bob Sweet)

Great Western Castle Class 4-6-0 Locomotives in the Preservation Era

DAVID MAIDMENT AND BOB MEANLEY

AN IMPRINT OF PEN & SWORD BOOKS LTD.
YORKSHIRE – PHILADELPHIA

First published in Great Britain in 2023 by
Pen & Sword Transport
An imprint of Pen & Sword Books Ltd.
Yorkshire - Philadelphia

Copyright © David Maidment and Bob Meanley, 2023

ISBN 978 1 39902 266 8

The right of David Maidment and Bob Meanley to be identified as authors of this work has been asserted by them in accordance with the Copyright, Designs and Patents Act 1988.

A CIP catalogue record for this book is available from the British Library.

All rights reserved. No part of this book may be reproduced or transmitted in any form or by any means, electronic or mechanical including photocopying, recording or by any information storage and retrieval system, without permission from the Publisher in writing.

Typeset in Palatino by SJmagic DESIGN SERVICES, India.
Printed and bound in India by Replika Press Pvt. Ltd.

Pen & Sword Books Ltd. incorporates the Imprints of Pen & Sword Books Archaeology, Atlas, Aviation, Battleground, Discovery, Family History, History, Maritime, Military, Naval, Politics, Railways, Select, Transport, True Crime, Fiction, Frontline Books, Leo Cooper, Praetorian Press, Seaforth Publishing, Wharncliffe and White Owl.

For a complete list of Pen & Sword titles please contact:

PEN & SWORD BOOKS LIMITED
47 Church Street, Barnsley, South Yorkshire, S70 2AS, England
E-mail: enquiries@pen-and-sword.co.uk
Website: www.pen-and-sword.co.uk

Or

PEN AND SWORD BOOKS
1950 Lawrence Rd, Havertown, PA 19083, USA
E-mail: Uspen-and-sword@casematepublishers.com
Website: www.penandswordbooks.com

All royalties from this book will be donated to the Railway Children charity [reg. no. 1058991] [www.railwaychildren.org.uk]

Other books by David Maidment:
Novels (Religious historical fiction)
The Child Madonna, Melrose Books, 2009
The Missing Madonna, PublishNation, 2012
The Madonna and her Sons, PublishNation, 2015
The Reluctant Traitor, PublishNation, 2021

Novels (Railway fiction)
Lives on the Line, Max Books, 2013
Steamy Stories, PublishNation, 2021 (Short stories)

Non-fiction (Railways)
The Toss of a Coin, PublishNation, 2014
A Privileged Journey, Pen & Sword, 2015
An Indian Summer of Steam, Pen & Sword, 2015
Great Western Eight-Coupled Heavy Freight Locomotives, Pen & Sword, 2015
Great Western Moguls and Prairies, Pen & Sword, 2016
Southern Urie and Maunsell 2-cylinder 4-6-0s, Pen & Sword, 2016
Great Western Small-Wheeled Double-Framed 4-4-0s, Pen & Sword, 2017
The Development of the German Pacific Locomotive, Pen & Sword, 2017
Great Western Large-Wheeled Double-Framed 4-4-0s, Pen & Sword, 2017
Great Western Counties, 4-4-0s, 4-4-2Ts & 4-6-0s, Pen & Sword, 2018
Southern Maunsell Moguls and Tank Engines, Pen & Sword, 2018
Southern Maunsell 4-4-0s, Pen & Sword, 2019
Great Western Granges, Pen & Sword, 2019
Cambrian Railways Gallery, with Paul Carpenter, Pen & Sword, 2019
Great Western Panniers, Pen & Sword, 2019
Great Western Kings, Pen & Sword, 2020
Great Western & Absorbed Railway 0-6-2Ts, Pen & Sword, 2020
Drummond's L&SWR Passenger & Mixed Traffic Locomotives, Pen & Sword, 2020
Southern 0-6-0 Tender Locomotives, Pen & Sword, 2021
LNER 4-6-0 Locomotives, Pen & Sword, 2021
Midland & LMS 4-4-0s, Pen & Sword, 2021
Great Western Castle 4-6-0 Locomotives, 1923-1959, with Bob Meanley, Pen & Sword, 2022
Great Western Castle 4-6-0 Locomotives, The Final Years, 1960-1965, Pen & Sword, 2022

Non-fiction (Street Children)
The Other Railway Children, PublishNation, 2012
Nobody ever listened to me, PublishNation, 2012

Other books by Bob Meanley **Non-fiction (railways)**
LMS Locomotive Profile No 11 – The Coronation Class with David Hunt, Bob Essery, Fred James and John Jennison, Wild Swan, 2008
Great Western Castle 4-6-0 Locomotives, 1923-1959, with David Maidment, Pen & Sword, 2022

CONTENTS

Preface & Acknowledgements 6

Introduction 8

| Chapter 1 | The Preserved Castles in BR service, 1965-1967 9
| Chapter 2 | 4073 *Caerphilly Castle* 30
| Chapter 3 | 4079 *Pendennis Castle* 36
| Chapter 4 | 5029 *Nunney Castle* 70
| Chapter 5 | 5043 *Earl of Mount Edgcumbe* 76
| Chapter 6 | 5051 *Earl Bathurst* 120
| Chapter 7 | 5080 *Defiant* 132
| Chapter 8 | 7027 *Thornbury Castle* 136
| Chapter 9 | 7029 *Clun Castle* 141

Appendix 161

Index 163

PREFACE & ACKNOWLEDGEMENTS

Great Western fans are fortunate that so many of their locomotives ended their days in the Woodham Brothers scrapyard at Barry and were thus available for rescue and restoration. Eight Castles survive – three preserved straight out of traffic at their withdrawal from service – 4073, 4079 and 7029. Five more have been recovered from Barry, four of them restored to operation – 5029, 5043, 5051 and 5080 – with just one still awaiting overhaul and restoration – 7027. The amount of material available has made it possible to produce this volume purely about these eight preserved locomotives. I am particularly grateful to Richard Croucher who gave me access to his files on 4079, including the full story of its time in Western Australia and its return to the UK, and to Drew Fermor for the telling of its overhaul since; to Peter Chatman and Mick Dean for much of the material about the restoration of 5051 and Adrian Knowles for some of the photographs from the *Great Western Echo* magazine. Bob Meanley has written the chapters on the overhaul and restoration of 5043, 5080 and 7029 and supplied many of the photos illustrating these chapters.

I am also grateful to Paul Shackcloth, who gave me access to photos in the Manchester Locomotive Society archive and allowed me to use them free of any publication fee as I am donating, as is my custom, all the royalties to the Railway Children charity (www.railwaychildren.org.uk) which I founded in 1995 and which supports street and runaway children picked up on railway and other transport terminals of the world – at the current time in India, East Africa and the United Kingdom. I have tried to trace and contact the copyright holders of all the photographs but if I have missed anyone, please get in touch with the publisher so I can make amends.

I am also grateful to John Scott-Morgan, friend and Commissioning Editor of Pen and Sword, Carol Trow my editor and Janet Brookes and the Pen and Sword design, production and marketing team for their encouragement, support and professionalism. I commend the book to all those who have enjoyed seeing or travelling behind these locomotives in their preservation years, some who may remember them in BR days and to those of you still looking forward to the experience of hearing, seeing and smelling these magnificent beasts once again.

My last Castle run before the end of BR steam was with 7029 on the special train from Preston to Carlisle to Hellifield on 14 October 1967. In the preservation era, I have had many runs with 4079, 5029, 5043, 5051 and 7029, the most recent being with 5043 on the 'White Rose' from Tamworth to York on 12 December 2015. I cover their story up to 2020 when unfortunately the coronavirus lockdown caused a hiatus in my personal acquaintance with the Castles, although it allowed me the time to complete all three volumes about them. I have tried to establish the current situation of each of these machines in the autumn of 2021. I look forward to meeting 4079, 5029, 5043, 5051 and 7029 once again – and possibly 5080 too. Perhaps looking towards 7027 is being too optimistic at my age!

David Maidment
May 2023

Due to a certain age difference, I never had the good fortune to have many of the experiences of Castle class engines which David enjoyed, and I have to confess that I never saw one on Old Oak Common shed in steam days, but I have had the immense good fortune to have become deeply involved with half of the remaining examples for a period of over thirty-five years. Having been born in LM West Coast territory at Tamworth, I grew up watching Coronations, Princesses, Scots, Jubilees and many others large and small. The fascination with Castles started at Christmas 1957 with the arrival of a Hornby Dublo *Bristol Castle*, and quickly accelerated with the discovery of the magical place known as Birmingham Snow Hill station. My involvement with preserved steam started in 1967 and for quite a period mostly centred around LMS locomotives, until being drawn into the then Birmingham Railway Museum via Jubilee *Kolhapur*. Of course, it was impossible not to become involved with all of the Castle class engines which were there at that time, and for almost forty years they have now become very familiar acquaintances. At Tyseley, we have been fortunate to muster sufficient facilities to give a small rendition of a true locomotive works, and more importantly have managed to assemble a young but highly skilled team to operate it. That has not been an easy task because it has to be remembered that in order to replicate the sort of major overhauls which Swindon carried out in the hundreds every year, it is necessary to possess access to every skill, machine and tool which Swindon possessed, otherwise the task is impossible. It was not achieved overnight and owes much to many people. Firstly, to Pat Whitehouse whose connections made the establishment of Tyseley possible, and to Jim Kent, whose huge engineering foresight lead to the establishment of the first workshop and the acquisition of essential machines and tools which are still in use every day. Of course, none of this could have happened so successfully without the many former railwaymen, engineers, managers, enginemen and artisans who gave their time and passed on their knowledge in order to ensure the long-term survival of steam. Without all of them there would be no section in this book on returning many of the surviving Castles to steam; indeed, all we might have had was a cold 4073 in a museum somewhere to look at and wonder.

We also need to acknowledge the contribution made by those who ensured that necessary technical information, particularly drawings and specifications, survived and perhaps the foremost of these was the late Ernie Nutty, who seemed to take every opportunity to download his encyclopaedic knowledge of Great Western locomotives and Castles in particular. It is safe to say that what remains of this technical information has never been so easily accessed and that is due in no small measure to the efforts of the custodians of the Great Western Society's collection, overseen for many years by Ted Lacey and more recently Kevin Dare.

Speaking as someone who began to understand the Castles just as the last of them were disappearing, it has been a privilege to have been able to have become so deeply involved with them to the point where they are daily acquaintances, and to have been able to gain so much first-hand knowledge of just what magical machines they really are. But time moves on. It has now been fifty-six years since 7029 was withdrawn from traffic, and yet it is still working and being looked after by a new generation who were born long after the end of BR steam, gratifyingly led by my son Alastair who has become a true Castle aficionado. There are also other young men championing the cause with 4079 at Didcot, 5029 at Crewe, and 7027 at Loughborough, so it does appear that the final chapter on the working history of the Castle Class may still be some way off. Long may that continue.

Bob Meanley
May 2023

INTRODUCTION

The pioneer, 4073 *Caerphilly Castle*, was restored and sent to the Science Museum in May 1960 and 4079 *Pendennis Castle* and 7029 *Clun Castle* were purchased from active BR stock in the 1960s. In subsequent years, 5029 *Nunney Castle*, 5043 *Earl of Mount Edgcumbe*, 5051 *Earl Bathurst*, 5080 *Defiant* and 7027 *Thornbury Castle* have all been rescued from the scrapyard and their story from the end of steam in BR service to the current time of writing (2021) is covered in this book. Earlier volumes published in 2022 by Pen & Sword, *The Great Western Castle Class 4-6-0s, 1923-1959* and *The Great Western Castle Class 4-6-0s, The Final Years 1960-1965*, cover their design, construction, operation and performance in Great Western and British Railways (Western Region) days and an assessment of their performance and impact on express locomotive development in the UK was summarised in the second of these.

Since the extinction of the class in regular BR traffic at the end of 1965, they have continued to demonstrate their prowess not just on their former own territory but have expanded their realm on many railtours and special workings to the North Wales Coast, the Northern Fells of both Shap and Ais Gill, Scotland East and West Coast, the East Coast Main Line and the Southern Region to Salisbury. One (5043) has replicated 5000's 1926 experience by appearing at Euston, another (7029) recalled memories of 4079 in 1925 at King's Cross. 4079 spent twenty-three years in one of the remotest areas of Western Australia. They have returned for overhaul at Swindon Works and in the private heritage railway workshops at Tyseley and Didcot.

They have performed with distinction on the main line too, not satisfied with the records broken in traffic in the 1930s and 1950s. Despite some initial problems with foreign coal, they have excited train performance enthusiasts with such exploits as 5043 beating 7029's record Plymouth-Bristol record of 1964 or its epic runs over Shap and Ais Gill, including producing the highest power output ever recorded by a Castle when storming over Ais Gill summit with over 500 tons in October 2010, with a calculated edhp of 2,030 – in terms of power per square foot of grate, the highest ever recorded by a British locomotive. Then again, recreating the *Bristolian* of the late 1950s running the 118 miles in 109 minutes 58 seconds (106 net) without exceeding 80mph. Rivalry between the Tyseley restored engines is to be anticipated now that 7029 has been returned to traffic and we look forward to it being planned to run over the Shap and Ais Gill routes to see if it can match or even beat 5043's achievements. And it will be interesting to see if a single chimney Castle, 5080, can equal the power and speed of the double-chimney pair of Castles when Tyseley have had the opportunity to give it an equally thorough overhaul.

The effort and achievement of these momentous performances is due to many people, especially the bands of volunteers led by Drew Fermor, Peter Chatman and Richard Croucher at Didcot and Bob and Alastair Meanley at Tyseley. Their stories are told here too, by Bob himself and by the Didcot people through access to their files and articles written in their own magazine, the *Great Western Echo* and other media.

Chapter 1
THE PRESERVED CASTLES IN BR SERVICE

7029 *Clun Castle*, the last Castle in BR service, was formally withdrawn in December 1965 but was observed on a few Banbury freight turns at the beginning of January 1966. It was a busy engine in 1965, however. After its triumph on the 9 May 1964 Ian Allan special, it was well occupied with a number of railtours and valedictory events as well as occasionally gracing the 4.15pm Paddington-Banbury. Known 1965 railtours were:

24 January: *Farewell to Castles* Birmingham–Bristol via Oxford & return via Stratford.

6 February: *Western Venturer* Paddington–Gloucester–Birmingham–Worcester–Paddington.

27 March: *Lickey & Midlands* Paddington–Worcester-Nottingham-Market Harborough-Bletchley-Princes Risborough-Paddington.

3 April: *Warwickshire Railway Society* (WRS) Special Birmingham-Southall-Swindon-Oxford-Worcester-King's Norton.

1/2 May: *Talyllyn AGM special* Shrewsbury-Paddington (overnight).

23 May: *Bulleid Pacific Railtour* Westbury-Bath-Cheltenham-Worcester-Birmingham.

12 June: *Sunday School Special* Cheltenham-Weston-super-Mare-Cheltenham.

5 Sept: WRS *Hants & Dorset Railtour* Banbury-Basingstoke & Weymouth-Reading-Banbury. The last run up the Berks & Hants by a Castle in BR service.

27 Nov: *Farewell to Steam BR-WR* Paddington-Bristol-Gloucester-Swindon.

4079 *Pendennis Castle* had been repaired and purchased by Mike Higson following its May 1964 withdrawal and ran some railtours, preserved, but before the 1968 end of BR steam and the steam 'ban'. 7029 *Clun Castle* also continued working on special trains and was active until November 1967. The railtours were:

4079 – 1965
8 August: *Ian Allan Railtour* Paddington-Worcester-Cheltenham-Paddington.

9 August: *Ian Allan Railtour* Paddington–Worcester-Swindon.

25/26 Sept: *Talyllyn AGM Special* Paddington-Shrewsbury & Tyseley-Paddington.

2 October: *Pendennis Castle Special* Paddington-Exeter-Paddington.

20 October: *Paddington Steam Farewell* Paddington-Worcester-Cheltenham-Paddington.

7029 – 1966
12 June: *LCGB Railtour* Stourbridge-Banbury.

24/25 Sept: *Talyllyn AGM Special* Banbury-Shrewsbury, Shrewsbury-Banbury.

12 Nov: *Shakespearian Railtour* Banbury-Stratford- Stourbridge Junction-Banbury.

4079, 7029 – 1967
4 March: 4079, *Birkenhead Flyer* and 7029, *Zulu*, two trains, Didcot/Banbury – Chester & return.

5 March: 7029 *SLS railtour* Tyseley-Birkenhead-Birmingham Snow Hill.

9/10 Sept: 7029 *Gainsborough Model Railway Society* Newcastle-Peterborough & Peterborough-Newcastle-Peterborough.

17 Sept: 7029 *Ian Allan Special* King's Cross-Leeds-King's Cross.

30 Sept: 7029 *Splendour of Steam Special* Peterborough-Leeds-Carlisle.

8 October: 7029 *Silver Jubilee* King's Cross-York-King's Cross.

14 October: 7029 *LCGB Castle to Carlisle* Preston-Carlisle-Hellifield.

In August 1965 4079 headed a light 6-coach 215-ton Ian Allan railtour to Worcester and back via Gloucester. Being a Sunday, there were engineering delays en route to Oxford, but 4079 touched 85mph at Honeybourne. It was even faster on the return, as after climbing to Sapperton Tunnel at a steady 34mph (25 per cent cut-off and ¾ regulator), it let fly with 90-93mph between Minety and Purton. It continued at 82mph before the Didcot stop and touched further 80s at Pangbourne and Ealing. I was a passenger on a railtour to Exeter and back in October 1965 when, with 310 tons gross, it climbed to Savernake at a minimum of 62mph and touched 76 at Lavington before running into Westbury nearly five minutes early. It topped Brewham summit at 59mph, touched just over 80 at Bruton, 78/74 at Somerton and 85 at Curry Rivell Junction before checks through Taunton and a 20mph p-way slowing at Victory Sidings, then the climb to Whiteball was surmounted at 41mph. After a tour to Totnes and the South Devon Railway with 4555 and 3205, 4079 returned to London from Exeter via Bristol. It took things easily early on following the 4.30pm Penzance and then ran with more vigour at 70-73mph across the levels through Bridgwater to Bristol. It was further delayed by signal checks and p-way slacks to Swindon but was regaining time with sustained 75/76mph running from Shrivenham to Didcot before a signal failure brought the train to a stand at Moreton Cutting. After a Reading stop, 4079 had the train up to 81mph by Taplow, but further signal checks between Southall and Paddington made the train very late into Paddington.

7029 was particularly active at this time and I joined several of its railtours and show logs of some of the most interesting in the tables below:

Lickey & Midlands Railtour, 27.3.1965
7029 *Clun Castle* – Old Oak Common
9 chs, 308/330 tons

Miles	Location	Times	Speeds		Gradients
0	Paddington	00.00		T	
9.1	Southall	14.10	62/sigs 53*	1 L	
18.5	Slough	22.42	74	1 L	
24.2	Maidenhead	27.20	78	¼ L	
<u>36</u>	<u>Reading</u>	<u>38.38</u>		1¼ E	
0		00.00		T	
5.5	Pangbourne	08.27	61		
12.5	Cholsey	14.42	72		
16.8	Didcot East Jcn	20.15	35*	1¾ E	
20.1	Culham	24.20	60		

The Preserved Castles in BR service • 11

Lickey & Midlands Railtour, 27.3.1965
7029 *Clun Castle* – Old Oak Common
9 chs, 308/330 tons

Miles	Location	Times	Speeds		Gradients
22.3	Radley	26.35	69		
27.4	Oxford	32.54		2 E	
0		00.00			1 L
3.9	Yarnton	06.54	46/54	2 L	1/240 R
16.5	Charlbury	19.11	65		L, 1/315 R
21.1	Kingham	24.39	67/64	½ E	1/402 R
28.5	Moreton-in-Marsh	31.32	61	1½ E	1/355 R
	Aston Magna Sdgs	-	52*		
33.5	Chipping Campden	37.07	64/59		1/151 F, 1/154 R
38.6	Honeybourne	41.07	85/72*	3 E	1/100 F
41	Littleton & Badsey	43.10	78		
43.1	Evesham	45.19	58*	4 E	
49.2	Pershore	50.54	72		
57.2	Worcester	59.41		5¼ E	
0		00.00		1 L	
5.6	Droitwich	09.40	52/sigs 5*/ pws 35*	5¼ E	
10.5	Bromsgrove	21.50/23.07		7¼ E/11 E	D6938 banker
13.8	Blackwell	29.18	28/26 ½	14¾ E	1/37¾ R
15	Barnt Green	31.55	42/52	15 E	
20.5	King's Norton	40.25	sigs 5*	12½ E	1/301 F
	Landor St Junction	54.03/60.40	sig stand	8¼ E	
26.9	Saltley Junction	64.10/65.23	sig stand	5½ E	
32.7	Water Orton	72.38	70	7¼ E	L
42.1	Tamworth	81.27	75/80	15½ E	
	Wichnor Junction	87.26	pws 60*/ pws 45*		
55	Burton-on-Trent	94.47	10*	17 E	
59.8	Repton	101.28	65		
66	Derby	110.42		20 E	
0		00.00		21 E	
2.3	Spondon Junction	08.57/14.50	sig stand		
2.9	Spondon	16.56/17.10	sig stand		

		Lickey & Midlands Railtour, 27.3.1965		
		7029 *Clun Castle* – Old Oak Common		
		9 chs, 308/330 tons		
Miles	Location	Times	Speeds	Gradients
4.1	Borrowash	20.44	pws 15*/48	
	Sawley Junction	28.30	25*	7 E
9.6	Trent	31.50	10*	6½ E
13	Beeston	38.15	42	
<u>16.3</u>	<u>Nottingham Midland</u>	<u>45.25</u>		<u>4 E</u>
0		00.00		½ L
6.7	Trent	12.15	51/10*	1¾ L
12.3	Hathern	22.25	5* (Flooded track)	
15.1	Loughborough	27.07	52	10½ L
20	Sileby	33.03	53	6½ L	1/508 R
<u>27.6</u>	<u>Leicester</u>	<u>43.54</u>		<u>6¼ L</u>
0		00.00		3 L
3.5	Wigston Magna	06.27	58		1/199 R
10	Kibworth North	12.48	60		1/161 R
12.8	East Langton	15.46	78		1/130 F
	Great Bowden Box	20.47/21.30	sig stand	
16	Market Harborough	24.00	15*	T
	Kelmarsh	32.21	50	1¾ E
	Lamport	37.32	40*	
	Pitsford	46.59	46/pws 10*	
0	Northampton	58.50/62.57	sig stand	10 E/6 E
3.3	Middleton	-	44		1/200 R
6.1	Roade	74.52	10* to ML	9 E
11.2	Castlethorpe	81.48	74/pws 10*	
19.3	Bletchley	98.05/109.14 water stop		2 L/13 L
	Winslow	120.39	64	
	Verney Junction	123.55	pws 28*	14 L
	Claydon (LNE) Jcn	130.00	10*	11 L
	Grendon Underwood	135.15	58	11 L
	Akeman St	138.02	76	

Lickey & Midlands Railtour, 27.3.1965
7029 *Clun Castle* – Old Oak Common
9 chs, 308/330 tons

Miles	Location	Times	Speeds		Gradients
	Ashendon Jcn	142.50/150.20 sig stand		19¼ L (waiting two Up Birminghams)	
	Haddenham	157.00	60 ½/58		1/200 R
	Princes Risborough	164.51		23 L	
0		00.00	sigs 2*	26¼ L	
3.2	Saunderton	07.11	36/50		1/88 R, 1/100 R
5.9	West Wycombe	11.12	63/ sigs 25*		
8.2	High Wycombe	16.08	25*	31 ½ L	
13	Beaconsfield	22.00	62		1/225 R
17.3	Gerrards Cross	25.48	82		
19.9	Denham	29.05	sigs 40*/ sigs 25*		
24.4	Northolt Junction	-	68	34 L	
26.9	Greenford	38.15	75	33½ L	
33.4	Westbourne Park	44.40			
34.7	Paddington	48.22		31 L	

This was a marathon effort on absurdly easy timings, remarkable for the performance of WR crews on foreign territory, the excessive number of p-way slacks encountered and the stamina of 7029 after a day of continuous steaming. It is a pity that the punctuality was spoiled at the end of the day by the inability to pick up water at Castlethorpe troughs because of a 10mph restriction there and then the loss of path, the WR not only allowing the 6pm Birmingham to precede but also a returning football excursion. Then in March 1967, I booked to join one of the two specials planned to mark the end of through passenger services from Paddington to Chester and Birkenhead. I chose to travel on the first one to be hauled by 4079 from Didcot to Chester and back.

The Birkenhead Flyer – Didcot-Chester
8.25am Paddington-Birkenhead, 4.3.1967
4079 *Pendennis Castle*
11 chs, 373/410 tons

Miles	Location	Times	Speeds		Gradients
0	Didcot	00.00		¼ E	
3	Culham	06.26	52		
5.4	Radley	09.21	54/60		

The Birkenhead Flyer – Didcot-Chester
8.25am Paddington-Birkenhead, 4.3.1967
4079 *Pendennis Castle*
11 chs, 373/410 tons

Miles	Location	Times	Speeds		Gradients
10.3	Oxford	15.18	45*		
12.7	Wolvercote Jcn	18.54	56		
16	Kidlington	21.50	58/62		L
19.7	Tackley Box	-	62		1/210 R
21.1	Heyford	29.13	69 / sigs 10*		1/266 F
28	Aynho Junction	37.37	63/60*/66		
33.2	Banbury	43.54		7½ E	
0		00.00	sigs 10*	½ E	
3.6	Cropredy	08.16	46/55		1/179 R
8.8	Fenny Compton	14.31	65/pws 40*		
	Fosse Road	22.20	77		
19.8	Leamington	27.46	sigs 15*	5 L	
21.8	Warwick	29.49	55/47		1/114 R
26	Hatton	35.52	42		1/103 R, 1/110 R
30.2	Lapworth	44.53	pws 10*		
32.7	Knowle	49.05	51	9 L	
39.9	Tyseley	56.46	69/pws 15*		
	Bordesley	63.55	sigs 5*/pws 15*		
43.1	Birmingham Snow Hill	66.58		13½ L	
0		00.00		13 L	
	Swan Village	09.39	54*		1/95 F
10.9	Priestfield	17.46	sigs 15*/ sigs 5*		
12.6	Wolverhampton	24.05		17 L	
0		00.00		17 L	
4.8	Codsall	08.05	pws 30*		
9.2	Cosford	13.00	74		1/137 F
12.5	Shifnal	16.05	55 ½		1/150 R
15.4	Hollinswood Box	19.57	42		1/150 R
16.7	Oakengates	21.18	64/sigs 30*		

The Birkenhead Flyer – Didcot-Chester
8.25am Paddington-Birkenhead, 4.3.1967
4079 *Pendennis Castle*
11 chs, 373/410 tons

Miles	Location	Times	Speeds		Gradients
19.6	Wellington	25.08	30*	13 L	
21.3	Admaston	27.25	60/sigs 20*/59		
	Upton Magna	35.17	sigs 20*		
26.1	Shrewsbury	42.45		16½ L	
		00.00		14 L	
3.7	Leaton	08.26	30/42		1/100 R, 1/240 R
11.7	Haughton	-	68		1/132 F
18	Gobowen	24.17	52	15 L	1/156 R
25.4	Ruabon	32.54	63/46		1/143 F, 1/83 R
30.2	Wrexham	39.42	sigs 20*/ sigs 15*	16½ L	
	Gresford	44.27	52*		
38.3	Balderton	-	74		1/82 ½ F
40.5	Saltney Dee Jcn	51.41	sigs 15*/sigs 15*		
	Chester South	56.51/58.09	sig stand		
42.3	Chester	62.29		17¼ L	

The second train (*The Zulu*), to commemorate the last day of through working between Paddington and Birkenhead, was headed by 7029 and made very similar times. The return journey with 4079 and the same load set off nearly 13 minutes late from Chester and gained two minutes to Wrexham with a strong climb of the 4-mile Gresford bank (1 in 82½), minimum 26½mph. A p-way slack to 15mph at Chirk dropped a couple of minutes which 4079 then recouped with speed in the high 70s from Rednal to Leaton. After overtime at Shrewsbury, 4079 left 15 minutes late, climbed the 1 in 120 past Admaston at 56mph and the 1 in 132/220 to Hollinswood at 42 followed by a swift acceleration to 82 down to Shifnal. A two minute gain to Wellington was then more than lost by a severe p-way slowing at Cosford and Wolverhampton was reached 17 minutes late. Two severe p-way slowings at Moor Street and Bordesley followed by a two minute dead stand at Small Heath and a further check at Lapworth made the train 24 minutes late, but a minimum of 52 at Fosse Road and 70 at Cropredy brought the train into Banbury 16 minutes late. A brisk run from Banbury to Wolvercote Junction (72 maximum at Bletchington) and an absurd amount of recovery time brought the train through Oxford on the centre road on time despite two momentary checks outside the station and Didcot was reached over a minute early. Both engines performed faultlessly but the schedule timed for the day did not seem to take the planned speed restrictions into account.

In the autumn of 1967, the preserved 7029 had gauging trials in the north–east and ran a number of specials on the East Coast main line and then on the two routes to Carlisle.

Miles	Location	Times	Speeds		Gradients
		King's Cross-Leeds, 17.9.1967, Ian Allan Railtour			
		7029 *Clun Castle* – Tyseley			
		8 chs, 276/290 tons			
0	King's Cross	00.00		T	
	Belle Isle	02.05			1/107 R
2.6	Finsbury Park	06.45	34/sigs 5*		
	Hornsey	10.31	57/sigs 20*		
	New Southgate	14.48	pws 5* to RL		
	Oakleigh Park	19.12	pws 10*		
12.7	Potters Bar	26.31	49½ / pws 15* to ML	½ L	1/200 R
17.7	Hatfield	33.47	78/pws 5*		1/200 F
	Welwyn Garden City	38.37/40.32 sig stand			
22	Welwyn North	44.45	pws 30*		
23.5	Woolmer Green Box	46.58	52		1/200 R
26.7	Langley	-	78		
28.6	Stevenage	54.05	sigs 10*		
31.9	Hitchin	59.50	58/sigs 10*	3 L	1/200 F
35.7	Three Counties	63.60	76		1/400 F
	Arlesey	64.56	80		
41.1	Biggleswade	68.05	77		
44.1	Sandy	71.23	sigs 30*		
47.5	Tempsford	74.20	75		
51.7	St Neots	77.52	74		1/330 R
56	Offord	81.34	78/67*		
58.9	Huntingdon	84.09	76	5 L	
62	Leys Summit	-	63		1/200 R
	Connington North	93.29	82/pws 15*		
69.4	Holme	95.31/96.32 sig stand			
75	Fletton Junction	109.22	sigs 30*/ sigs 5*		
<u>76.4</u>	<u>Peterborough</u>	<u>113.54</u>		<u>7 L</u>	To New England for water
0		00.00		25 L	
	Westwood Junction	-	sigs 15*		
3.1	Werrington Junction	06.27	56		
8.4	Tallington	12.05	60/56/ sigs 40*		
12.2	Essendine	18.41/19.05 sig stand			

King's Cross–Leeds, 17.9.1967, Ian Allan Railtour
7029 *Clun Castle* – Tyseley
8 chs, 276/290 tons

Miles	Location	Times	Speeds	Gradients	
20.7	Corby Glen	30.31	58		
23.7	Stoke summit	34.06	52/sigs 40*		
29.1	Grantham	39.51	75	33 L	
33.3	Barkston South	44.45	sigs 40*/64		1/200 F
	Claypole	49.05	84		
43.7	Newark	52.42	75	32 L	
	Muskham	-	pws 50*		
	Carlton	-	75/78		
	Dukeries Junction	62.25	69		1/200 R
	Gamston	-	83		1/178 F
62.2	Retford	68.24	62*	30 L	L
67.5	Ranskill	73.14	76		
	Bawtry	77.11	pws 40*		
	Black Carr Jcn	-	sigs 30*		
		86.37/86.58 sig stand			
		89.25/90.00 sig stand			
<u>79.6</u>	<u>Doncaster</u>	<u>93.48</u> (76 net)		<u>37¾ L</u>	

7029 ran on to Leeds in 41½ minutes net, arriving 23 minutes late. The train returned south leaving Leeds 26 minutes late (late stock to platform) and Doncaster 21 minutes late and ran superbly from Doncaster to Peterborough in order to connect with the last Up Hull.

0	Leeds	00.00		26 L	
29.8	Doncaster (pass)	47.12		21 L	
	Rossington	53.00	67		L
	Bawtry	56.44	pws 40*		
41.9	Ranskill	60.57	69		
47.2	Retford	65.48	66*		
	Askham Tunnel	-	65		1/178 R, 1/200 R
	Dukeries Junction	72.33	80/84		1/200 F
	Carlton	76.14	82		L
	Muskham Troughs	-	60*		

Miles	Location	Times	Speeds		Gradients
65.7	Newark	82.41	68/76		L
	Claypole	-	75		
76.1	Barkston South Jcn	90.27	72		1/200 R
	Peascliffe Tunnel	-	pws 30*		
80.3	Grantham	95.48	58		
85.7	Stoke Summit Box	101.59	55		1/200 R
88.7	Corby Glen	104.43	75		1/178 F
97.2	Essendine	111.30	79		1/200 F
	Helpston	116.49	77/82		L
	Westwood Junction	122.51/124.28 sig stand			
<u>109.4</u>	<u>Peterborough</u>	<u>126.15</u>		<u>13 L</u>	

After replenishing with water, 7029 left Peterborough just two minutes late and ran competently enough without any more fireworks, the best being 57 minimum at Stevenage, 65 at Knebworth and 77 at Welwyn North. However, with two 15mph p-way slacks and a signal check at Belle Isle, we took 91 minutes, arriving 11 minutes late, an anti-climax. Being a Sunday, there were many slacks for track renewal, and 7029's acceleration from each on both outward and return journeys was extremely rapid. After Peterborough southbound, 7029 was not pressed initially as standing for an hour had caused the fire to clinker badly, but this was sorted out by St Neots.

A month later, 7029 had moved to Preston on the West Coast main line, where it took over a railtour starting from Liverpool with 9F 92091. It had a light train of only seven coaches, but it was a spirited run, highlights below from Lancaster to Shap summit:

9.15am Liverpool Exchange-Carlisle, 14.10.1967, LCGB Railtour
7029 *Clun Castle* – Tyseley
7 chs, 214/235 tons

Miles	Location	Times	Speeds		Gradients
0	Lancaster (Castle)	00.00	55*	4½ L	
3.1	Hest Bank	02.41	78		
6.3	Carnforth	05.23	60*	T	
	MP 9½	-	48		1/134 R
13.6	Milnthorpe	12.53	66		1/173 R
19.1	Oxenholme	19.09	50	2½ E	1/111 R
22.6	Hay Fell	-	46		1/104 R
	Lambrigg Crossing	25.42	48		1/131 R
26.2	Grayrigg	28.26	44		1/106 R
	Low Gill	-	pws 40*		
32.2	Tebay	36.14	58	7¼ E	L
35.2	Scout Green Box	39.58	44		1/75 R
37.7	Shap summit	43.44	47	9¾ E	1/75 R

Shap station was flooded and 7029 crept through the water and was stopped by signals at Eden Valley Junction but was still, due to generous recovery time, over ten minutes early into Carlisle. The railtour returned to Hellifield and I show the log after the water stop at Appleby and attention to brakes of the rear coaches which were rubbing.

4.20pm Carlisle-Liverpool via Hellifield, 14.10.1967

7029 *Clun Castle*

7 chs, 214/235 tons

Miles	Location	Times	Speeds		Gradients
0	Appleby	00.00		17½ L	
2.5	Ormside	04.06	62		1/176 F
5.3	Griseburn	07.08	57		1/100 R
7.5	Crosby Garrett	09.23	58½ / 62½		1/100 R, 1/166 R
	Smardale	-	64		L
10.7	Kirkby Stephen	12.41	57/53½		1/100 R
14	Mallerstang	16.41	49/54		1/100 R, 1/330 R
17.5	Ais Gill	20.55	48	10½ L	1/100 R

Recovery time then put 7029 and its train on time at Ribblehead and with easy running, no more than 72mph down past Horton-in-Ribblesdale, we were 10 minutes early into Hellifield where 92091 took over for the run back to Liverpool. Less than a year later regular steam working disappeared from British Railways' tracks, and the future of these two Castles – and six others – lay in the preservation era.

7029 *Clun* Castle, in private ownership, but still in BR steam days, spent a few days on the Eastern Region in September 1967. It is powering the *Splendour of Steam* railtour from Peterborough to Carlisle, tackling a violent side gale at Blea Moor, 30 September 1967. The special returned to Peterborough with A4, 4498 *Sir Nigel Gresley*. (John Whiteley)

7029 *Clun Castle* at Shap summit with steam to spare on the Liverpool-Carlisle LCGB railtour of 14 October 1967. (Author's Collection)

7029 *Clun Castle* at Nottingham (Midland) depot after working the first leg of the Ian Allan *Lickey and Midlands* railtour of 27 March 1965. (F.K. Davies Collection/John Hodge Collection)

7029 *Clun Castle* at Bristol Temple Meads before departure for Swindon on the Western Region's *Farewell to Steam* special, 27 November 1965. (Bruce Oliver/Rail Archive Stephenson)

7029 *Clun* Castle at Swindon at the end of the Western Region's *Farewell to Steam* special, 27 November 1965. (Bruce Oliver/Rail Archive Stephenson)

The privately owned 4079 *Pendennis Castle* on Sapperton Bank with an Ian Allan railtour, 8 August 1965. (W. Potter/MLS Collection)

4079 *Pendennis Castle* passing Ranelagh Bridge with an Ian Allan railtour to Worcester returning via Gloucester to Swindon, 9 August 1965. (R.C. Riley)

4079 *Pendennis Castle* worked the first of two railtours between Didcot and Chester to mark the end of steam on the GW route from London to Birkenhead. It was named *The Birkenhead Flyer* and 4079 is seen here on shed at Chester being prepared for the return journey, 4 March 1967.
(N.H. Spilsbury/MLS Collection)

4079 *Pendennis Castle* on the return *Birkenhead Flyer* climbing Gresford Bank, 4 March 1967.
(A.C. Gilbert/MLS Collection)

The Preserved Castles in BR service • 25

A few minutes later, 7029 *Clun Castle* with the second of the Ian Allan specials, *The Zulu*, climbing Gresford Bank, 4 March 1967. (A.C. Gilbert/MLS Collection)

The following day 7029 repeated the trip with a Stephenson Railway Society railtour from Tyseley to Birkenhead. There was so much demand for this that a relief was run, 7029 working the main train down and returning on the relief back to Snow Hill, seen here passing through Hooton station on the return, 5 March 1967. (A.C.Gilbert/MLS Collection)

7029 *Clun Castle* spent a couple of months on railtour duties in the north in September and October 1967. After checks on route availability, 7029 hauled its first railtour on the East Coast main line for the Gainsborough Model Railway Club from Newcastle to Peterborough, seen here at Newark Northgate on 9 September 1967. It operated a similar trip on the following day. (R.O. Tuck/Rail Archive Stephenson)

The Preserved Castles in BR service • 27

7029 *Clun* Castle at Holbeck shed, Leeds, during its Ian Allan railtour from King's Cross to Leeds and back, 17 September 1967. (MLS Collection)

7029 *Clun* Castle sets off from Leeds through Beeston on the return leg of its King's Cross-Leeds railtour, 17 September 1967. (MLS Collection)

7029 *Clun* Castle at Newlay & Horsforth, Leeds, with the King's Cross-Carlisle railtour of 30 September 1967 which it worked from Peterborough to Carlisle via the Settle & Carlisle line. The railtour returned to Peterborough behind 4498 *Sir Nigel Gresley*.
(A.C. Gilbert/MLS Collection)

7029 *Clun* Castle worked a Preston-Carlisle-Hellifield LCGB railtour, 14 October 1967, and is seen here departing from Carlisle Petteril Bridge.
(L. Riley/MLS Collection)

7029 *Clun* Castle at Petteril Bridge with the LCGB railtour, 14 October 1967. (L. Riley/MLS Collection)

7029 *Clun* Castle at a photo stop at Appleby on the Carlisle-Hellifield leg of the LCGB railtour, 14 October 1967. (The photographic position was protected by stewards and the BT Police.) (David Maidment)

Chapter 2
4073 CAERPHILLY CASTLE

4073 *Caerphilly Castle*, the doyen of the class, was built in August 1923 and exhibited at the British Empire Exhibition at Wembley in 1924. It spent most of its career at Old Oak Common, and in the 1950s, at Bristol Bath Road. Although slated for withdrawal in 1955, its last Heavy General overhaul took place in the autumn of 1956, and it was not withdrawn from Cardiff Canton shed until May 1960. Its final mileage was 1,910,730, at 52,000 average per annum over its 37-year life in active service. It was made part of the National Collection and was theoretically just cosmetically restored at Swindon (although the Works Manager is said to have authorised a full overhaul) before being formally handed over to the Director of the Science Museum by Dr Beeching at Paddington station in June 1961. It was hauled by road to the National Science Museum on 4 June and displayed in the transport section, before moving in 1996 for three years to the Great Western Railway Centre at Didcot and finally in December 1999 to its current position at STEAM Museum, Swindon.

The original unaltered Castle pioneer, 4073 *Caerphilly Castle*, recently ex-works in 1958 at Canton shed. This was its last Works visit before withdrawal in 1960 and preservation, initially in the Kensington Science Museum and subsequently at STEAM Museum in Swindon.
(John Hodge)

4073 *Caerphilly* Castle on arrival at Paddington with the 8.15am (SO) Abertillery-Paddington, 27 March 1959.
(Brian Stephenson)

4073 at Caerphilly Works Yard after a casual repair, 19 October 1959. It was withdrawn seven months later from Canton depot.
(E.R. Mountford/F.K. Davies & John Hodge Collections)

I was in the Divisional Passenger Train Office in June 1961 and was given the tip and slipped out to photograph the restored 4073 being propelled into Paddington station by a diesel shunter 'D4004' for the formal hand over by Dr Beeching to the Curator of the Science Museum, 2 June 1961. (David Maidment)

4073 on the buffer stops of platform 4 at Paddington ready for the hand over by Dr Beeching to the Director of the Science Museum, 2 June 1961. (David Maidment)

4073 *Caerphilly Castle* • 33

4073 is conveyed by a Pickfords. Scammell 6-wheel tractor into Kensington Church Street from Notting Hill Gate en route to the Science Museum, 4 June 1961.
(Brian Stephenson)

34 • GREAT WESTERN CASTLE CLASS 4-6-0 LOCOMOTIVES IN THE PRESERVATION ERA

4073 *Caerphilly Castle*, with the *Cheltenham Flyer* headboard mounted on the front of the Castle hauling the train in the 1930s, at STEAM Museum, Swindon. (STEAM Museum)

4073 *Caerphilly* Castle on display at STEAM Museum, Swindon. (STEAM Museum)

Chapter 3
4079 PENDENNIS CASTLE

The story of 4079's preservation, twenty-three years in Australia and subsequent repatriation to the United Kingdom is told with the help of records in two 2-inch-black folders provided to me by the then Deputy Chairman of the Didcot based Great Western Society, Richard Croucher, and updated on restoration work since 2000 by GWS member Drew Fermor.

4079 was the seventh Castle built at Swindon Works in February 1924, and named *Pendennis Castle*, after a fortification built in 1539 near Falmouth in response to threats to the south coast from France and Spain at time of Henry VIII. The letters of its nameplate were taken from the nameplate of the withdrawn Dean 'Duke' of that name of 1895. The locomotive cost £5,565, including £1,359 for the boiler, plus £1,250 for a new 3,500 gallon tender. During its first year it ran 65,669 miles and was selected for the 1925 exchange with the Gresley pacifics as, along with 4074, it had the reputation of being one of the best of the early Castles. It was given a thorough overhaul before the trial to ensure its perfect condition and spent a week at King's Cross running local turns using Yorkshire hard coal whilst Driver Young and his fireman familiarised themselves with the route and East Coast operations. The LNER authorities tried to insist that its sixteen coach 500 ton trains were banked through the two tunnels up Holloway Bank to Finsbury Park, but Driver Young refused and astounded the LNER officials and loco crews with its clean and rapid starts, passing Finsbury Park on every occasion under six minutes, a good minute faster than its rival Gresley pacifics, and causing a number of local enginemen to lose their wagers. It ran 1,257 miles during the exchange. Its overall performance for which it was celebrated was recounted in detail in my first volume about the Castles, *Great Western Castles, 1923-1959*. Driver Young summed it up at the end and is quoted as saying, 'Taking the test as a whole, I feel that neither of the three of us, my engine, my mate or myself, were extended to the full and I always felt if necessary I had a little in hand.'

Unfortunately relations between the two companies were soured by the subsequent publicity when the *Great Western Magazine* published an account pointing out the GW engine's superiority, but the GW Chairman, Sir Felix Pole, allowed a set of drawings of the Castle valve gear and sanding apparatus to be sent to Doncaster, and lessons were learned, the Gresley pacifics subsequently being equipped with a higher boiler pressure, long travel valves and a more efficient sanding gear.

After the exchange, 4079 replaced 4073 as the exhibit at the Wembley exhibition from May to November 1925 and only failed to earn a medal as it did not comply with the requirement to be constructed of 100 per cent British materials – it had Belgian steel tyres! 4079 then unusually moved to many different GWR depots during its career, including Old Oak Common, Bristol Bath Road, Wolverhampton Stafford Road, Gloucester, Cardiff Canton and finished its last few months at Swindon. It was one of the three selected engines (and the only one of the 1923-27 batch) for the May 1964 high speed railtour but was withdrawn from Westbury depot where it resided after losing some of its fire as the firebars collapsed after the fire burned too brightly on its speedy performance to that point. It was officially condemned after a total recorded mileage of 1,758,398 (to December 1963), but it had only run 38,000 miles since its previous 'Heavy Intermediate' overhaul, which was between August and October 1961.

Mike Higson, the owner of the Roundhouse Bookshop in Northwood and a fireman at Crewe in the 1950s, had considered buying a 'Black 5' but then decided to purchase a double-chimney Castle or Royal Scot.

He was made aware of 4079 and its excellent condition and historical significance and was persuaded by buy that instead. 4079 was given a full (and unauthorised!) overhaul at Swindon in 1965, due to the enthusiasm and dedication of staff there, and its name and numberplates were rescued from a shed where they had been stored pending their preservation in a museum. 4079 had had no less than eighteen different boilers during its 40-year career. Its final one was 6672 built in December 1937 for rebuilt Star 5086 and its tender, Collett 2390, which had been built for King 6005 in 1927, was exchanged for the younger 2913, built for Hall 6954 in 1943. It was back in main line running order by August 1965 and ran a number of railtours on which it demonstrated the excellence of its repair, achieving more than 90mph on one of the trains. Between the tours it was stored at the Southall shed.

By 1967 Mike had some business concerns and decided to sell 4079

A last survivor that Mike Higson might have chosen, 4080 *Powderham Castle* – the last of the 1923-7 batch of Castles, equipped with new front end, 4-row superheater boiler and double chimney in August 1958 and not withdrawn until August 1964, seen unusually at Crewe North shed, where Mike had been a fireman, 1964. 4080 achieved the highest mileage of any of the Castles (excluding rebuilt 'Stars) – 1,974,461. (MLS Collection)

and it was purchased by John Gretton and Bill McAlpine and moved to Didcot from where it ran a number of further railtours including the last steam run to Chester over the former GWR route in March of that year. During the 1967-72 steam ban it was initially stored in the lifting shop at Didcot before moving to a former ironstone quarry engine shed at Market Overton, Rutland, in 1972, where it had access to the BR system. It joined in the main line operations of 'return to steam' in 1972 over the North & West line, based at Hereford. I joined one in April 1974 when it teamed up with a Gresley pacific once more, 4079 running the outward leg from Newport to Shrewsbury, 4472 *Flying Scotsman* returning. 4079 took the honours again running punctually with its 395 ton train, climbing to Church Stretton at 37mph minimum before a twenty minute delay outside Shrewsbury because of a derailment at Sutton Bridge Junction. 4472, admittedly with the extra weight of its second tender, struggled to Church Stretton, falling to 18mph because of shortage of steam, taking over an hour and a half to get to Hereford and not far short of three hours to Newport. By 1976, now owned solely by Bill McAlpine, 4079 was at Steamtown, Carnforth. 4079 ran several further trains before a boiler tube failed and it was stored there, withdrawn for overhaul.

4079 in Swindon Works after the 'unofficial' overhaul of 4079 prior to its purchase by Mike Higson, March 1965. (G. Wheeler/GW Trust)

4079 at Dauntsey during a running in test after its Swindon overhaul, 19 March 1965.
(Peter Rosier/GW Trust)

4079's test crew, with 4079 at Dauntsey. Second left is Bill Godsell, the foreman at Swindon Works who supervised the overhaul, 19 March 1965.
(Peter Rosier/GW Trust)

4079 at Worcester Shrub Hill with the Ian Allan Paddington-Worcester-Cheltenham-Paddington railtour, 8 August 1965. Bill Thorley, the WR Motive Power Officer who organised the selection for the 9 May 1964 Castle 'swan song', is standing on the running plate.
(Brian Penney)

4079 at Shrewsbury after working the Talyllyn Railway AGM special from Paddington and handing over to two 'Manors', 7802 and 7812, for the run to Towyn, 25 September 1965.
(MLS Collection)

4079 *Pendennis Castle* • 41

4079 backs down from Chester shed to the station for the return leg of the *Birkenhead Flyer* railtour of 3 March 1967. (GW Trust)

4079 at Steamtown, Carnforth, before the sale to the Hamersley Iron Company, 1976. (David Maidment)

Operation in Australia

In 1975, a few members of the Hamersley Iron company's Seven-Mile rail workshop formed the Pilbara Historical Railway Society and sought to acquire a steam locomotive to run on the company's 293 kilometre (183 mile) line to the ore mine at Tom Price and the 100 kilometre (62 mile) extension from Wombat Junction to Paraburdoo. Finding a standard gauge preserved locomotive in Australia was difficult – the only possibility was a 4-6-0 '3642' of the New South Wales Railway, but enthusiasts there were reluctant to see their engine several thousand miles away in the remote and inaccessible north west of the country. During a visit to the workshop of the UK parent company's managing director, Sir Russell Maddigan, the Society's wish was expressed and Sir Russell is reported to have said, 'I'll get you *Flying Scotsman*!' He approached Bill McAlpine who by then was the sole owner of 4079, and his response was 'You can't have *Flying Scotsman* but you can have *Pendennis Castle*.'

A contract was duly drawn up between the Hamersley Iron PTY Ltd. and the Steamtown Railway Museum Ltd. to whom Bill McAlpine had entrusted the engine and 4079 was sold for the bargain price of £90,000 subject to a number of stringent qualifications. The seller had to renovate 4079 to working order to the satisfaction of the buyer's inspection and provide spare parts – a set of firebars, brake shoes, and material for the replacement of the brick arch when needed. The list of repairs required to meet the demands of the contract included a renewal of both smokebox and superheater tubes, renewal of the front tubeplate, renewal of the firebox wall stays, the welding of pit holes in the boiler barrel and the rehabilitation of wasted sections in the petticoat and steam pipes. When these repairs had been completed, 4079 performed one last 'farewell' railtour in the UK on 29 March 1977 when it joined a train from Euston at Saltley and ran the special to Didcot and returned as far as Knowle & Dorridge. Dick Potts was the driver and described the journey in an article for *Railway World* in August 1977. 4079 took over the 13-coach 455 ton train from two class 20 diesels a few minutes late and although the coal was not the best – soft friable Welsh coal from Navigation Colliery – the southbound trip went well, Potts described 4079 as riding superbly, quiet, and springy although with a slight knock from the reverser as they coasted down Hatton Bank. Potts used 30 per cent cut-off, reduced to 25 per cent climbing to Fenny Compton passed at around 50mph (assessed as 4079's speedometer was wildly inaccurate). The lateness was reduced to 5 minutes by Banbury and Potts went hard out of there, roaring past Kidlington after recovering from Sunday single-line operations beyond Aynho and storming through Oxford on time on the middle road at 60mph. Potts was on the cushions for the northbound return run, but the inspector told him that the fire got badly clinkered and the resultant poor steaming to Banbury was sorted there while they waited for a late running Paddington-Birmingham express to pass. Sorted it was, as 4079 kept the tight 8-minute schedule from leaving Leamington to passing Hatton, the cut-off dropped to 50 per cent for the last quarter-mile, the exhaust reverberating round the English countryside for the last time for another forty-five years or more. Back at Tyseley, a volunteer had to remove 2ft of clinker from the grate! It left Avonmouth at the end of May on the MV *Mishref*, an Egyptian vessel registered in Panama, and arrived in Sydney in July 1977 when a 'Titan' crane was required with 150 ton lift capacity to bring 4079 out of the ship's hold.

Initially the locomotive was stored for several months at the Everleigh carriage workshops in NSW and on 8 April 1978 it was finally steam tested and towed the 104 miles to Newcastle by diesel electric loco 4516 where it was loaded onto the *Iron Baron*, a ship equipped with heavy duty lifting cranes. It was accompanied in the hold by three new 3,600hp diesel locomotives for the Hamersley Iron Railway. 4079 was unloaded at Dampier in Western Australia, at the western end of the railway and placed in the Six-Mile Museum while it was assessed for the changes needed to make it fit for operating on the line. The required modifications that were made were:

Fitting a proportional valve to control the air pressure brakes on the coaches

Provision of a 5,000 gallon gin water carrier to augment the 4,000 gallon tender

A smokebox mounted large electric headlamp to meet Western Australian regulations

A turbogenerator on top of the firebox to provide electrical power

Two UHF radios and antennae to link to the Hamersley line control

The isolation of the BR ATC equipment

The removal of the exhaust steam injector and provision of a new Gresham & Craven live steam injector (a second was fitted in 1981) as the GW ones were unreliable in the hot desert conditions.

The locomotive had to operate in very dry hot conditions (40° + in summer) and desalinated water was obtained from the company's power house in Dampier. By October 1978 two coaches had been obtained and with a third, painted dark green to match the locomotive. A Western Australian 5,000 gallon water carrier was modified for standard gauge use and a diesel compressor added to provide air braking for its train.

The route over which 4079 was to run special excursions was a heavy duty continuous welded track railway over which 180 wagon 23,000 ton iron ore trains, 1.7 km in length, ran 24 hours a day 364 days a year hauled by 3 x 3,600 hp diesel locomotives. The company's 48 diesel locomotives shifted 48 million tons a year of iron ore to the docks at Dampier. The line peaked at 2,450 ft at Mt Tom Price and the gradient was no more than 1 in 300 facing loaded ore trains westbound though there were stretches of 1 in 50 eastbound through the Chichester Ranges National Park between Dampier and Tom Price that would not unduly worry the three diesels and the ore empties. Between Wombat Junction where the spur to Tom Price forked and Paraburdoo in the Pilbara Range, the line dropped steadily at 1 in 200 for 60 miles and the three diesels on westbound ore trains required three more at the back as well. This section included an arched steel bridge 35 metres high over the Spring Creek.

4079 performed its inaugural run from the Seven-Mile workshop to Dugite for sixty school children in November 1978, but its first public trips were in 1980 to Tom Price and Paraburdoo, many just to the picnic site at Camp Curlewis, 60 miles from Dampier in the Chichester Range. Running up to 65mph on the level was achieved with ease. Getting suitable coal was difficult as the only steam coal was mined at Newcastle in New South Wales and cost A$16,000 (£6,400) to purchase and bring 50 tons to Dampier. Its performances on the 1 in 50 grades hauling three coaches and the water gin were excellent and in September 1981 there was a *Salute to Pendennis Castle* tour from Paraburdoo through to Dampier, supported by a 2,655 kilometre day trip (!) from Perth, with a flight to Paraburdoo, the 383 km run to Dampier and then flight back to Perth. Two crews were rostered for the trip, the temperature exceeded 50° in the cab and a relief train, diesel hauled, with additional coal and water followed the special, which also was required to stop and douse any fires started by sparks from 4079. Because 4079 had to work hard through the initial Pilbara Range, this facility was much used. Later in the descent from the Chichester Range, a speed of 84mph was recorded.

There were no trips in 1982 because of a shortage of crews available and subsequently the Society got permission from the drivers' trade union to allow volunteer drivers to be used which both saved money and allowed crews to work in addition to their rostered hours. Trips resumed in 1983, but 4079's superheater units failed and fourteen new double elements were installed in April 1983 after the winter season (specials did not run in the summer when the heat was excessive). Because of the rising cost of the fuel ($40 a ton at source, $240 after transport to Dampier) local brown coal was tried but was unsuitable and South African black coal was imported at $120 (£48) a ton but it caused 4079 steaming problems as the fire would clinker badly – the coal was creating 15 per cent ash content. Consideration was given to conversion to oil-firing but rejected as it could affect the life of the copper firebox. By 1984, problems were accumulating, an 11 inch crack in the blast pipe was uncovered and the engine was withdrawn for overhaul. The boiler was lifted in 1985, a new brick arch was built and the worn piston valves were replaced. The tender was also overhauled and a new tank manufactured. The overhaul was completed and the engine repainted in February 1987. It was in service again at the end of the summer in August 1987 and was hauling 310 ton trains to the Curlewis site. It had occasional use in 1988 but the highlight was the visit of *Flying Scotsman* to Western Australia during its 1988/9 visit to the country. The two British locomotives were to meet up at Perth on 17 September 1989 and then work together over ten days on the Westrail system, 4472 and 4079 double-heading trips in the Perth area, then on 30 September working together from Perth to Kalgoorlie with an overnight stop in Merriden (200 kms). The two engines then went further to Kambalda, where 4472 returned to Kalgoorlie while 4079 ran south on the 300 km line to Esperance on the shores of the Southern Ocean. Finally 4079 returned to Kalgoorlie. 4079 had been brought by road 1,200 kms from Dampier to Perth to take part in the 'meet'.

Trips continued in the early 1990s, but the iron ore traffic was building up and it was becoming difficult to find paths between the ore trains. By 1994 it was becoming evident that 4079 required a heavy overhaul. After its last run in October 1994 it was withdrawn as its boiler was declared unsafe, and the company commissioned an inspection and report from the Willis Light Engineering Pty Ltd. in January 1995. The report was detailed and listed the repairs needed, stating initially, 'Steam loco 4079 is in a

4079 leaves Didcot for its last run in the UK back to Tyseley on the railtour described by Driver Potts, 29 May 1977. (J. Reeves)

generally reasonable condition for its age and use. Although not properly maintained, it has been generally cared for, kept under cover and well-lubricated. The loco however requires a significant amount of work to bring it up to good and safe running condition, particularly in respect of the boiler, cylinder assemblies and brakes.'

The report listed four items on the tender requiring repair, sixteen items on the engine and motion and eleven on the boiler. Most were minor, but the major items were replacing the crown stays in the boiler, replacement of the 2in tubes, renewal of worn parts in the cylinder assembly and the need to identify the loss of brake efficiency. The cost was assessed at A$ 188,000 (£75,000) +transport, cranage, insurance and repainting. As the line was being resignalled with a full electronic system incompatible with a steam locomotive, the costs of this repair and making 4079 compatible was rejected and 4079 was retained on display only in the Pilbara Historical Railway Society's museum.

4079 on the deck of the Titan crane, Sydney Harbour, 14 July 1977. (Roundhouse Magazine/ GW Society)

4079 being lifted from the hold of the MV *Mishref* at Sydney Harbour, 14 July 1977.
(J. Beckhaus/GW Society)

NSW diesel 4516 hauls 4079 in light steam from Sydney to Newcastle, climbing Eastwood Bank, 27 March 1978.
(Roundhouse Magazine/ GW Society)

4079 *Pendennis Castle* • 47

4079 in the hold of the *Iron Baron* sandwiched between two new 3,600 hp diesel electric locomotives for the Hamersley Iron Company, en route to Dampier, 31 March 1978.
(Roundhouse Magazine/ GW Society)

4079 on display at Seven Mile Yard, Dampier, before modifications for running on the Hamersley Iron Railway, 22 April 1980.
(D.A. Finlayson)

4079 crossing the 35m high Spring Creek bridge with an excursion from Paraburdoo to Tom Price and Dampier, 27 September 1981.
(J. Dare/GW Society)

4079 and the standard Pilbara Historical Railway excursion train, 21 July 1984, before overhaul in the Hamersley workshop.
(J. Beckhaus/GW Society)

4079 on a Pilbara Historical Society excursion, 21 July 1984.
(John Lyas/GW Society)

4079 stops for passengers to dismount for photos and a picnic in the Chichester Ranges National Park at Curlewis, October 1984.
(John Lyas/GW Society)

4079 by the Fortescue River with the excursion train to Curlewis, 21 July 1984. 4079 was showing signs of problems with steaming that led to overhaul over the following three years.
(J. Beckhaus/GW Society)

4079 waits to pass a 23,000 ton ore train headed by three of the Hamersley Iron Company's diesels at Rosella, 21 July 1984.
(J. Beckhaus/GW Society)

4079 Pendennis Castle • 51

4079 crossing the high Spring Creek bridge, with diesel 3015 tucked inside, 22 July 1984. (J. Beckhaus/GW Society)

4079 after overhaul among Hamersley Iron Company's diesels at Dampier, c1987. (Lindsay G. Morrison/GW Society)

4079 halts in the Chichester Range National Park with a Society excursion train, after its overhaul, c1987.
(Lindsay G. Morrison/GW Society)

During the 10-day meet up in Western Australia between 4079 and 4472, the two engines ran trips around the Perth area before the long double-headed venture to Merridin, Kalgoorlie and Kambalda. Here 4079 and 4472 *Flying Scotsman* run parallel with each other at Northam, about 60 miles east of Perth, 24 September 1989.
(Gary Merrin/Steam Railway)

4079 Pendennis Castle • 53

4079 during one of the 10/11 September 1994 excursions to celebrate the 70th anniversary of *Pendennis Castle*, shortly before its withdrawal and storage at Dampier.
(GW Society)

4079 after withdrawal and standing at Dampier awaiting a decision on its possible repair and future use, Autumn 1994.
(Railway Magazine)

Repatriation

The question arose of what to do with 4079 and one of the Pilbara Society drivers, Peter Ward, contacted the *Railway Magazine* and its Editor at the time, Nick Pigott, and suggested that someone in the UK might try to repatriate 4079. At around the same time, Adrian Lumley-Smith, an expat working for Rio Tinto Zinc Ltd. in their Perth, Western Australia Office, knowing that his colleagues at Hamersley Iron were beginning to feel that 4079 was starting to become a bit of a problem, had been trying to persuade Rio Tinto that it should be returned to the UK. Adrian led the negotiations for Rio Tinto which resulted in the selection of the Great Western Society as the best place to return 4079. A 'Castle' in original condition was too good an opportunity to pass up and negotiations began with Rio Tinto in October 1998 and were finally concluded towards the end of the following year. A number of British organisations had been interested including Andrew Goodman who owned a heavy haulage company used for road movement of rail vehicles around the UK and the 6024 Preservation Society, but the choice of the Great Western Society site at Didcot was strongly supported by Andrew Scott, Director of the National Railway Museum. Rio Tinto agreed to donate the locomotive to the GWS at Didcot; the GWS just had to collect it!

The deed of gift from the Hamersley Iron Pty Ltd. and the Great Western Society was dated 6 April 2000 and was on condition that the Society preserved and restored it to working order. It was to be collected from the Seven-Mile railway workshop and to be removed by the end of June 2000. The Society was to arrange a full mechanical and boiler examination as soon as it was at Didcot and the cost of restoration assessed. The Society was to use its best endeavours to raise that amount and start the renovation as soon as possible. There was no commitment to restore to main line standards but to consider this if the additional cost could be raised.

In anticipation of the agreement, the Society started a search for a shipping company that would return the locomotive at affordable cost. First approaches to shipping lines brought estimates ranging from £80,000 to £150,000. In one case, the Society was quoted £125,000 in the hold of a monthly scheduled service from Sydney to Marseilles which could call at Port Dampier specially and was then told that the tide and currents off Port Dampier were very strong and docking could be delayed and the cost would go up at £10,000 for every 24 hours delayed either going in or out of port. Air transport on a Russian Antonov heavy transport plane would be quick but was ruled out when the £350,000 cost was quoted. Then valuable assistance was given by Steve Smith of the Premier Forwarding Ltd. Company of Ipswich who found Wallenius Wilhelmsen Lines had roll-on/roll-off ferries that undertook world haulage and could transport 4079 in the hold without the need to lift the engine. It could be loaded on a road hauled 'maffei' (a rubber-wheeled trailer) and pushed on and off the vessel. The cost was just £41,000 and with the road haulage from Dampier to Freemantle, where one of the line's ships called, and insurance, the total cost was estimated at £50,000. Andrew Goodman, who himself had been interested in acquiring 4079, agreed to arrange haulage from Portbury Dock, Bristol to Didcot free of charge.

The GWS set about fundraising and simultaneously made an application to the Heritage Lottery Fund for a grant. Citing the historical value of the engine and its 1925 performance that had influenced British locomotive design plus the fact that Didcot was on the UNESCO World Heritage GW Paddington-Bristol main line, the grant application was processed in a record four days by HLF and an award of £37,300 towards the agreed final cost of £49,842 was agreed, the rest coming from the GWS appeal. The grant was on the understanding that the locomotive would be returned to Didcot by the end of July 2000, and the grant would expire at the end of August. A suitable vessel was identified, the *Toba*, leaving Melbourne which would call at Freemantle in April 2000 and was due in Bristol on 7 July, having been routed via Singapore, Hong Kong, Yokohama, Los Angeles, the Panama Canal, Miami, New York, and St John's, Nova Scotia. Richard Croucher and the GWS General Manager Mick Dean visited the locomotive at Freemantle to ensure 4079 was properly prepared, greased against corrosion at sea, and secured for the voyage after its road trip from Dampier by Wesfarmers Transport. There was a slight hiccup and extra cost of £800 when the local dock union insisted that cranage from the road trailer to the maffei on the dockside must be handled by their unionised staff. The Australian National Cultural Committee made no objection to its export (if the locomotive had been in the country for thirty years or more, they could have claimed it as an Australian heritage artifact) and there were no problems from the Australian Customs authorities. Julie McWhirter, the company's project officer for external affairs, smoothed the way, even being advised by the Customs authorities to check with the Australian Ministry of Defence that they had no objections!

The hand-over ceremony from Hamersley Iron Company to the GWS took place on the North Quay at Freemantle on 19 April 2000 with the Executive Chairman of Hamersley Iron, Chris Renwick, and Phil Knife, the Vice-President of the Pilbara Historical Railway Society, in attendance. Removable items such as the number and nameplates, whistles, gauges and the safety valve bonnet were returned on a BA 747 air freighter at a cost of A$830. The 20,000 mile round-the-world journey started three days late on 25 April 2000. It eventually arrived after the first circumnavigation of the world by a Castle a day late on 8 July at Portbury Dock, Bristol and customs clearance was completed on the 10th – the boiler tubes were carefully checked to ensure no drug smugglers had taken advantage of the engine at any of the far eastern docks and also that no dangerous Australian spiders had hitched a lift (not a laughing matter!). It was then hauled by Andrew Goodman's company via the M4 to Didcot where it arrived on 14 July, a fortnight before the planned celebration at Didcot when 4079 was lined up with other locomotives outside the shed and 1338, 3738 and sister Castle, 5051 *Earl Bathurst*, were in steam. Members of the Pilbara Historical Railway Society and staff of the Rio Tinto Zinc Company were awarded life membership of the GWS. 4079 had travelled 5,000 miles in Western Australia during its twenty-three years in the Outback.

GWS Deputy Chairman Richard Croucher and General Manager Mick Dean in the smokebox of 4079 during degreasing and other preparation for its voyage, at Perth before movement the following day to Freemantle Dock, 17 April 2000. (GW Society)

4079 being conveyed by road from Perth to Freemantle North Wharf, 18 April 2000. (A. Bollans/ GW Society)

4079's engine and tender arriving at the North Wharf, Freemantle, 18 April 2000. (Don Finlayson/ GW Society)

4079 Pendennis Castle • 57

4079 on arrival at the North Wharf, Freemantle, 18 April 2000.
(Don Finlayson/GW Society)

4079 after the formal handover from Hamersley Iron Company to the GW Society in a ceremony at North Wharf, Freemantle, 19 April 2000. The name and numberplates were fixed for the ceremony but removed afterwards for air-freighting to the UK. (Don Finlayson/ GW Society)

4079 being lifted from the road trailer to the maffei at North Wharf, Freemantle, ready to be rolled onto the ferry *Toba*, 19 April 2000. (A. Bollans/GW Society)

4079 on the maffei at North Wharf ready for greasing and checking by Richard Croucher and Mick Dean before loading onto the *Toba*, 20 April 2000. (Richard Croucher)

4079 being hauled by tractors out of the roll-on/roll-off ferry *Toba* on the maffei at Portbury Dock, Bristol, 8 July 2000. (Adrian Knowles)

4079 after unloading from the *Toba* at Portbury Dock, awaiting road haulage by Andrew Goodman's haulage firm to Didcot, 10 July 2000. (Adrian Knowles)

4079 *Pendennis Castle* on display at the Great Western Centre, Didcot on the Open Day to welcome its return, 30 July 2000. (Adrian Knowles)

The line-up of GW express power outside the Didcot engine shed, 4079, 5051 *Earl Bathurst*, 6024 *King Edward I*, 5900 *Hinderton Hall* and 6998 *Burton Agnes Hall*, 30 July 2000. (Adrian Knowles)

Richard Croucher and Sir William McAlpine with the painting of 4079 by Barrie A.F. Clark that was the first prize in the draw fundraising for 4079's restoration, 30 July 2000. (G. Bewes/GW Society)

Second Restoration

Pendennis Castle was home, but the Great Western Society had undertaken to repair and restore it to working order. The first obligation was to examine it and identify the repairs, major and minor, that would need to be resourced and funded. It was clear that 4079 was in a rundown condition. Its last Heavy Intermediate repair at Swindon was in mid-1961 and its last Heavy General overhaul was back in 1959, and 4079 had run over 140,000 miles since. Although significant repairs to engine and boiler had been undertaken in Australia between 1984 and 1987, the engine had been stored out of action for over six years and the climate, abrasive wind and sand had damaged surface and the motion. Didcot had the knowledge of the major repairs identified in 1994 by the engineering consultants employed by the Hamersley Iron Company and the GWS met in 2001 and 2002 to plan the way forward, and to begin the task of raising what would be a significant amount of cash.

The boiler was lifted in May 2002 and the frames transferred into the Works. In August, Drew Fermor was asked to lead the restoration and the immediate plan in September was for 4079 to be dismantled and the wheels to be cleaned and then go away for reprofiling, the frames to be cleaned, MPI testing to take place, general derusting and the motion area to be degreased and painted. Four Working Parties would then be needed to concentrate on the following areas:

1) Cylinders
2) Brake rigging
3) Vacuum system
4) Bogie assembly

A request would be made to the 'Heavy Mob' who were restoring 3822 and 7202 to assist with making the boiler and firebox cleating and machining parts of 4079's motion, with funds raised for 4079. The tender did not need so much attention, the tank having received major repairs in Australia in 1983. The engine needed to be restricted to an overall height of 13ft 1in to conform to the BR loading gauge, but with the full weight on the loaded springs, fortunately no cutting down of the chimney and boiler mountings was necessary. The bogie and driving wheels were reprofiled at Tyseley in October 2003.

There was debate within the GWS about the livery to which 4079 would be finished. The options considered were:

1) 1925 livery as for the LNER trials
2) As currently painted with red frames and exhibition GW finish
3) Plain green with GW roundel
4) Photographic grey for one year
5) Go to GWS membership for choice of GW livery
6) Any GW livery as suggested by a GWS member who would sponsor the cost.

The BR green liveries were not considered, despite the fact that this was the livery most members will have seen 4079 wearing. The GWS Council recommended option 2, with the possibility of option 4 for a year. An appeal for the funds to overhaul 4079, estimated at £100-120,000, was launched in April 2004.

Work continued on its chassis, axleboxes remetalled and the locomotive was placed back on its wheels in March 2006. The bogie was reassembled in January 2007. The smokebox saddle was removed and sent away for a specialist repair. The Australian injectors were replaced by standard GWR designed injectors. After the initial work, an assessment was made in May 2008 of the costs necessary to complete the restoration:

New cylinder and valve liners:	£ 31,000
New valve & piston rings	£ 8,000
Renewal of small boiler tubes	£ 8,000
Renewal of large boiler tubes	£ 7,000
New tender wheel tyres	£ 8,000
TPWS & OTMR for ML working	£ 20,000
VAB audit & test running	£ 17,500
Total	£ 99,500

Another appeal for funds was made in 2009 and the situation in December of that year was that the following work had been completed:

Cross-heads and connecting rods had been refitted
  Inner big ends and new white metal surfaces
  Tender near complete, water scoop removed

Boiler in final stage of re-staying

Repaired smokebox saddle refitted.

£60,000 had been spent and a further £40,000 was required for the tube work and the valve and cylinder liners. The original valves from 5051 had been replaced and were in store and were retrieved for use with 4079's new liners. A new ashpan was completed and new boiler cleating rolled in 2010. The work however was protracted – as well as the delay in raising the necessary funds alongside other projects underway at Didcot for which also appeals for funds were being made, the volunteers available for work on 4079 were restricted to weekend working, basically just alternate Saturdays, so that the restoration has taken much longer than originally envisaged. In March 2020, with further delays caused by the coronavirus pandemic and the government lockdown rules, there was still the pipework to do, but the end was in sight and it was anticipated that the first steaming of 4079 would take place in the autumn of 2021.

The overall cost of repatriation and subsequent restoration carried out entirely by volunteers was £300,000. The intention at this stage is to use the engine for heritage line work only. Restoration to main line running standards will be considered if and when the necessary funds are available, but it faces competing demands for resources from many other expensive preservation projects.

The boiler of 4079 is fired for the first time since its return to the UK. Deputy Chairman Richard Croucher has the honour of bringing the locomotive back to life, 3 October 2020. (GW Echo)

Above left, above right and opposite: After out of frames steam test in October 2020, the boiler of 4079 is lifted back into the frames at Didcot Railway Centre's workshop, 7 November 2020. (*GW Echo*)

The words above give a factual description of the work and funds necessary to restore 4079 once again. However, one of the Great Western Society volunteer members, Drew Fermor, who was (and is) Project Manager, has written his personal experience and that of his team and he has kindly agreed to allow me to use his words to complete the story of 4079's return to life at the beginning of the third decade of the twenty-first century.

The Second Restoration (as described by Drew Fermor, 4079 *Pendennis Castle* Project Manager):

When the fanfare of her triumphant return to the U.K. in 2000 had subsided, the cold hard reality of having to bring this engine back to life had to be dealt with. In theory it should be easy - right? It hadn't been in a scrapyard so was relatively complete. It hadn't steamed for about 6 years but it had steamed relatively recently in the scheme of things. In a famous and oft used phrase, 'how hard can it be?'

Well...

The first thing to remember was that the locomotive had been in use, on and off, since 1965. Her last Heavy General overhaul was in 1959 and when Mike Higson bought her in

1964, Swindon gave the engine a good going over too. He got much more than he paid for as this was the last Castle through Swindon. Stories of the copper pipe store being well stocked one day and mysteriously empty the next with a well appointed No. 4079 sat in the works is often told... There was the work prior to her departure in 1977 and a number of fairly large jobs done in Australia. She was well looked after. However, a full overhaul hadn't been undertaken in all that time. No matter how well built your steam engine is - and Castles are *extremely* well built - time and mileage will eventually exact their revenge

66 • GREAT WESTERN CASTLE CLASS 4-6-0 LOCOMOTIVES IN THE PRESERVATION ERA

4079 after overhaul and repainting at Swindon following purchase by Mike Higson, 11 April 1965. (W. Potter/ MLS Collection)

on the machine. The more that was dismantled, the more that was discovered that was either worn out, broken or, in a few cases, no longer fitted with G.W.R. parts. The engine was best described as 'very, very tired'. And very sandy. Along with *Pendennis* came buckets of red sand. Behind every crevice where grease collected, so did the sand. The last of it I found underneath a small piece of metal that was part of the electrical conduit on the smokebox we missed in May 2021! We have had everything apart, inspected and repaired it where needed.

One of the main things we as a team decided early on was that as so much of the locomotive was still essentially Swindon material (I'm not using that loaded word 'original') that wherever possible, that Swindon material should be restored. As a result, No. 4079 isn't a 'showroom fresh' restoration. For example, take a look at the brass trim that runs up the edges of the cab entrance on each side. While we have made them fit properly and ensured they are secure, you can also see all the dents and dings caused by all the countless people climbing up and down over decades of operation. Things like this are the very 'soul' of the machine and it was *so* important for us to retain that patina. Also, that vexed question of livery was settled early on. She has worn the GREAT [crest] WESTERN livery since her entry into preservation in 1965. It's not our place to change that either. There is a magnificent photograph of her waiting to be handed over to Mike Higson in 1965 outside 'A' Shop. It became the aim. So much so, it's hung over my sofa at home! So, how do you get there? Let me take you on a virtual tour of the locomotive and I'll show you the highlights of what we've done!

The heart of any steam engine is the boiler, it's her power plant and it makes her live and breathe. This one dates back

to 1937 and was originally fitted to a Star conversion – No. 5086 *Viscount Horne* carrying No. 6672. We were lucky to have the services of long term Didcot boilersmith, Peter Gransden, assisted more recently by Ali Matthews, who has breathed life back into what was at best a curate's egg. The plate work is in relatively good condition considering its age. The practice in Australia was to drain the boiler when she wasn't being used and given the heat of the desert, this has helped immensely in its preservation. There were the usual seam rivets in the firebox, foundation ring rivets and a whole host of other bits and pieces. The worst bit was undoubtedly the crown stays which required replacing. A common repair that we are doing on our boilers is the replacement of the lower section of the dry extension – the bit where the smokebox is fixed on. This is exposed to all the ash, soot, heat, water and other stuff that eats into the steel over time and as the boiler is attached to the engine via this joint, we thought it prudent to make sure it was up to scratch! The most visible of the new material we have added is the boiler cladding itself. The old stuff really was too far gone and very rusted. This was a case of being pragmatic about the restoration and this was one bit that we had to give up on. The other section that was life expired was the ash pan and this again has been fabricated from new by the team.

Her wheels were basically in good condition. The tyres on all the loco wheels were capable of being turned and were sent off to Tyseley for re-profiling. The tender wheel tyres however were well down on their thickness. The good news was however that we had a spare set at Didcot so we sent these away with the loco wheels and had them serviced too. In the finest traditions of Swindon, the wheels that came off eventually had their tyres replaced and now sit under the replica of the special wide Hawksworth tender for No. 1014 *County of Glamorgan*. Painting these things is always a massive and seemingly thankless task. You go round the whole thing and think you are done until the next smart Alec walks past and spots a bit you missed. Then you turn the wheels and discover all the other bits you have missed… The wheel bearings were all refreshed with new whitemetal and machined to suit. The leaf springs were all sent away for refurbishment and these too were refitted upon their return.

Another area of concern was *Pendennis Castle's* cylinders. They had several problems that had to be addressed. The first of which was the large broken bit! There are four parts that make up the cylinders of a Castle. The inside cylinders which have their bores and valves and the engine's steam chest. It also has the front section of the saddle that holds the smokebox and the exhaust pipe flange. The two outside cylinders and valves are separate pieces that have their exhaust pipes exit through a hole in the frames. These exhaust pipes connect together and exit through a flange in the rear section of the saddle in the fourth section. It was the flange to which the two to one manifold that then has the blast pipe bolted on top that was broken. It had been welded in Australia but this had failed again. These are all made of cast iron so require specialist welding techniques. The only way that the company doing the work would guarantee it was if they could have it at their workshop. This meant removing the 5 cwt casting that is fixed in place with fitted bolts and that meant we had to produce a special tool to get them out! Once perfected, it took a day to get them all out. The next working session took all day to slowly cajole it out of position. When at the contractors, a new section was cast to fill in the missing section and then the whole thing was heated to a very high temperature. Then the welding was done and the whole thing cooled down very slowly. Another day pushing the component back into place and another day to get the rest of the bolts back in and you'd have never known we'd been there! Such is the life of a loco restorer… The bores of both the valve and cylinders were worn and new liners needed fitting. The cylinder drain cocks fitted were non-standard steam operated versions and a full set of brand new GWR designed units and their associated linkage was manufactured.

The bits to go in the refurbished cylinder block were next. The pistons were capable of being turned down to suit the new bores and the piston rods were skimmed to smooth out the wear. The valve rods were too worn but a company was able to recover them for us using a special spiral welding technique to build them back up again. The valve heads she had were half on the smaller 'A' size and half on the bigger 'B' size. Thankfully, our other Castle, No. 5051 *Earl Bathurst*, had its valves bored out to 'B' size and therefore we were able to make up a set of original Swindon 'A' size heads. All the rings were skimmed to suit the new bores and new brasses for the ends of the rods and the steam tight glands were made.

All of the whitemetal bearings in the rods, eccentrics and cross heads were renewed and machined. Some of the clearances in the motion brasses were at twice the scrapping clearance so they were all renewed too. One of the really interesting things about being able to be up close to such a historic machine is that you get to see all the history written across it. The most pleasing discovery was that two of the crankpin nuts are marked up as once being part of No. 4074 *Caldicot Castle* – her fellow 1925 trials competitor!

The locomotive's structure was in pretty good condition but there were a few parts that were in need of attention. The biggest of which was that which made up the drag box where the coupling between the locomotive and tender is made. This area receives a fairly unpleasant mix of steam locomotive by-products that all get washed down with water. This is all slightly acidic and will slowly eat through the steel plates that make up this complex area. If you draw a horizontal line about half way down the cab side number plates on both sides, most of the plate work from there down is new. The main frames were fine and thankfully so were the bits that were complex pressed shapes. The cab sides from the line up were preserved as there is a lot of detail on them that is from the engine's life so we kept it. We could have easily cut whole brand new cab sides but that's not the way we did things! The weld on the front is invisible. You can still see it on the back. That way, the story of what we have done is there to see. We have left our mark on her too!

All of the locomotive's systems have been thoroughly inspected and the biggest change was the injectors. The Australian injectors were fitted for very good reasons, but we don't think we are going to have to run in the desert again (!) so we went back to the GWR style live steam injectors. She should of course have an exhaust injector and a live steam injector but at the time this was done, the patterns for the exhaust injector didn't exist and we had access to a pair of live steam injectors. Perhaps that's the next bit to do for the following overhaul? The steam heat system was removed in Australia from the loco (but not from the tender) after the mason's valve but this was in poor condition too. This has all been remanufactured and replaced. She had a full complement of Swindon manufactured controls apart from that and, again, a long process of careful refurbishment was undertaken. Nearly all of that pipework fitted by the guys at Swindon in 1964 / 1965 was still there but there were a few bits that were modified for the new injectors and a few other bits that were no longer serviceable. Again, replacements were made and fitted.

Her tender is a wartime build and although it was one of the newer bits of the engine (1942!), it still needed all the same plate work repairs to the drag box as the locomotive did. Apart from that, the rest of the tender was in pretty good condition. The tank had its baffles replaced in Australia. It was thoroughly cleaned internally and painted with a gooey bitumen coating to keep the rust at bay. Again, all the systems were carefully assessed, repaired and restored. The few modifications that have been done are low level fire hose style fillers added to the tank for convenience and the pipework above the water scoop removed so that we can get the largest possible volume of water in the tank. Marginal gains but gains none the less and not easily spotted either.

The hardest thing about the project was the decision we took a few years ago to stop pursuing the original project aim of taking the engine on the main line. There were a number of reasons for this. It was firstly the right decision for the Great Western Society. There is a level of commitment of funding, manpower and administration that is incumbent upon this kind of venture. It's right for some preservation groups. Right now, it's not the right time for us. It's a 'never say never' situation, but for the foreseeable future we have decided that this will be the way forward for our fleet. The amount of modifications required to the locomotive also weighed in on this decision. Being able to have a 'live' Castle presented as the GWR intended is indeed an appealing prospect. We have had an excellent response from the use of No. 6023 *King Edward II* on preserved lines and No. 2999 *Lady of Legend* has begun to cement this. These operations ensure that the loco is visible to a diverse audience and also provides more valuable income for the society than the fees we would receive for main line operation and helps us to keep the collection as a whole in operation and at least prepare for those inevitable bills for the 10 yearly overhauls. We have also found that we are able to give far better access to our locomotives for both us as volunteers and the general public. Undoubtedly, more people will get to ride behind the engine and sharing the collection with everyone is one of the most rewarding things we do.

So where we are now? As I write this, it's early June of 2021. We have been through the trials and tribulations of 2020 which greatly delayed proceedings. I myself was kept away from Didcot for a great deal of the previous year in which we had planned to finish the engine due to the Covid 19 pandemic. Some of the team were still able to make it to the loco works and they kept the project ticking over. I have been really fortunate to have such an amazing crew. I saw her recently and there was a beautiful coat of gloss green paint beginning to emerge on that new boiler cladding. Closer and closer to that 1965 picture... It's not long now and readers will now know more of the subsequent history than I can from where I sit now! We will soon light the fire, wind the reverser to full forward, pull the whistle chain and open the regulator. She will then move under her own power again for the first time since 1994. This will finally close a circle that opened on that day in 1977 when she was coaled and watered at Didcot in that final rail tour before heading down under, allegedly, never to return.

I am very grateful and privileged to have been such a big part of No. 4079's history over the last approximately 20 years. I hope that now she is emerging from the works, a great many more people get to enjoy her. We have a lot of fun to come for a great many people - not just us and that's an amazing privilege to be able to provide that too. However, the greatest privilege has been to work with the Great Western Society members who I have met and become great friends with whilst working on *Pendennis Castle*. She has brought together a disparate bunch of really hard working and dedicated individuals who have stood by me and the locomotive through thick and thin. My team are the very best I could have hoped for. Some of them even started as teenagers and have grown up as the project has come to fruition. The reason I started at Didcot was because I am fascinated by the locomotives. The reason I stay is for the friendship of those whom I work with. Therefore, the only appropriate way to finish is to say something to all of them, some of whom are no longer with us and very much to our regret never saw No. 4079 completed. Thank you so very much.

Note: The boiler was steam tested in July 2021, the completed locomotive was on display with 5051 and 2999 at Didcot on 28 August 2021. The public launch of the completed engine finally took place on the 2nd April 2022.

Chapter 4
5029 NUNNEY CASTLE

5029 *Nunney Castle* was built in May 1934 and spent its first twenty-four years at Old Oak Common. It was withdrawn in December 1963 from Cardiff East Dock and sold to Woodham Bros. at Barry in 1964, where it resided until 1976 when it was purchased by a consortium led by Warwick Ormandy with the Great Western Society ultimately taking it on. It was restored to main line operation condition at Didcot and ran a number of main line specials in the early 1990s. David Maidment was present on a railtour to Stratford-on-Avon in November 1991 and 5029 made heavy weather of the first section to High Wycombe because of dragging brakes. 5029 was worked flat out (50 per cent cut-off, full regulator) on the climb to Saunderton falling from 40 to 34mph with a comment that brakes still appeared to be dragging. Signal checks and more sluggish running made the train 15 minutes late into Banbury where water was taken and the coach brake cords pulled and performance improved, the loss reduced to 3 minutes before further checks at Hatton North Junction. A much sprightlier run was made in October 2000 when 5029 worked a 10-coach *Ynys Mon Express* from Crewe to Holyhead with 76½ attained before Chester and a steady 78-82mph between Flint and Prestatyn to recover the loss of 12 minutes caused by a prolonged signal check at Saltney Junction. Llandudno Junction was reached just 5 minutes late. Floods and creeping at 5mph in Anglesey made the train 11 minutes late at Holyhead arriving in a gale-force headwind and torrential rain – as had been the case most of the way along the North Wales Coast. The return journey ironically was severely delayed taking water before departure because of a

5029 *Nunney Castle* easing past Royal Oak with the Up *Torbay Express*, 27 August 1960. (R.C. Riley)

defective fire hydrant – water everywhere except in the tank!

It was in the ownership of Barry Cordell and Mike Little before sale to Jeremy Hosking and after repair was returned to main line operation in 2008. In May 2014, on 9 May 1964 50th Anniversary Train of the Z48 high speed Castle specials, it ran the 75½ miles from Exeter to Bristol with an 8-coach 290/310 ton load in 70 minutes 22 seconds, covering the 40 miles from passing Taunton at 77mph to a stand at Temple Meads in 33 minutes 44 seconds. It left Exeter 4½ minutes late and after a slow start, passed Tiverton Junction 6½ minutes down at 65mph. Whiteball was cleared at 54½, then sustained high speed with 79 at Wellington, 81 at Creech, 81 at Bridgwater, 75 at Highbridge, 77 at Worle Junction, minimum 69 at Flax Bourton and a final 78 after, reaching Bristol exactly ½ minute early.

At the end of its boiler certificate in 2017, it was housed with Jeremy Hosking's collection at Crewe where it is currently (2021) awaiting overhaul in order to return to main line operation. It has been stripped down and the boiler is awaiting a new copper and steel firebox and upgrading from 2-row to 3-row superheater as fitted to the 1946 Hawksworth engines to enable it to cope better with the type of coal available today. Its frames are due for overhaul which will be started when work on 70000 *Britannia* is completed. The middle cylinder block has been removed and a new wooden pattern is being manufactured so that a new block can be cast. The tyres are in good order but the axleboxes need to be checked and – if found to be in good order – reassembled. The tender is away under overhaul, awaiting the fabrication of a new tank.

This will include modification at the front of the tender to allow the fitting of up-to-date safety systems required for current main line running.

The rusting form of 5029 in the scrapyard of the Woodham Bros. at Barry, 1965 and 9 June 1967. (D.K. Jones/MLS Collection & Brian Penney)

5029 *Nunney Castle* takes water at Llandudno Junction on a Crewe-Holyhead *Ynys Mon Express* railtour, 28 October 2000. (David Maidment)

5029 *Nunney Castle* and 5051 *Earl Bathurst* on the *Devonian* Finsbury Park-Plymouth railtour (although wearing the *Mayflower* headboard) near Taunton, 3 May 2003. The Castles worked from Bristol to Plymouth but 5051 failed at Laira and the 12-coach special returned to Bristol with 5029 piloted by a Class 47 to Newton Abbot. (Peter Gray/GW Trust)

5029 Nunney Castle • 73

5029 at the Great Western Centre, Didcot, 1 May 2010.
(David Maidment)

5029 on the turntable at the Great Western Centre, Didcot, 1 May 2010. The airbrake equipment is visible in this photograph.
(David Maidment)

5029 *Nunney* Castle and 6024 *King Edward I* climb from Bodmin Road to Liskeard over the East Largin Viaduct, with the *Cornish Riviera Express* railtour, 28 June 2010. (Adrian Knowles)

A panned shot of 5029 working on the West Somerset Railway. (Andy Taylor)

Chapter 5
5043 EARL OF MOUNT EDGCUMBE
(BOB MEANLEY)

5043 was built in March 1936 at a cost of £4,848 and named *Barbury Castle*. Renamed after a GWR director in September 1937, it spent much of its career at Old Oak Common, interspersed with a four-year stay in West Wales at Carmarthen. It finished at Cardiff East Dock from where it was withdrawn in December 1963. It was purchased from the Barry scrapyard in 1973 and taken to Tyseley where it was to be used as a source of spare parts for that depot's 7029. In 1996, it was decided to restore 5043 to main line running condition with double chimney and Hawksworth tender as it ran in the 1950s. It was complete for steaming in

Old Oak Common's 5043 at the head of the 11.10am Milford Haven at Cardiff General, c1959. (John Hodge)

5043 arrives at Swindon with a stopping service off the Gloucester line, c1961. (MLS Collection)

2008 and ran many railtours from 2008 to 2017, during which time it performed with great reliability and some spectacular running, details of which are included in the 'operations' section later. In preservation it has visited Liverpool, Manchester, Chester, Llandudno, Anglesey, Carlisle, Huddersfield, Lincoln, Ely, Edinburgh, Stirling, York, Euston and the West Coast main line and London Marylebone, as well as WR destinations such as Paddington, Plymouth, Bristol, Cardiff, Gloucester, Hereford and Worcester. It was withdrawn from traffic when its boiler certificate expired in 2018 and has almost completed its ten-year overhaul at Tyseley at the time of writing (November 2021), having successfully passed its boiler tests.

5043 last saw the inside of Swindon's famous 'A' erecting shop in April 1962 when it received a heavy intermediate repair and a newly repaired four row superheated boiler. It was destined to have little more than twenty months in traffic before its final withdrawal in December 1963, arriving in Woodham Brothers' Barry scrapyard around April 1964. It spent nine years at Barry and during that time it was turned into little more than the bare bones of a locomotive, being stripped for spare parts by a number of preservation organisations (including Tyseley) together with the attentions of metal thieves. Perhaps the biggest loss was the collection of connecting and coupling rods which had been loaded into the tender when the engine was prepared for movement from Cardiff East Dock. They are fully evident in photos of the engine in the early days at Barry but subsequently disappeared and remain missing to this day. A decision was taken at Tyseley in the early 1970s that it might be prudent to buy the mortal remains for spare parts, in particular it would provide a spare 4-row superheater boiler for 7029 as the only other loco so fitted. As I write this, it is interesting to note that 5043's boiler has just passed its hydraulic test after a ten year overhaul but has temporarily given up its superheater header to 7029 due to a problem arising with 7029's own header; the original purpose of buying 5043 has finally but partially come to fruition!

The engine was duly extracted from the scrapyard in 1973 and made a sorry sight upon its arrival at Tyseley. Despite the fact that it was not intended to restore the engine, many important parts were removed and placed in storage and the bearing surfaces of important parts were coated in thick preservative made to the special formulation of Chief engineer Jim Kent. That foresight was of greater importance than anyone would have assumed at the time. It took up residence at the end of the coal stage bank and became a prominent but frankly most unattractive feature of the works for around twenty years. Considering its very exposed and windswept location, it survived this period surprisingly well. It became something of an enigma with varying suggestions as to what might be done with it. Those suggestions ranged from removal of the boiler and scrapping the rest of it, rebuilding it with a No.1 Standard boiler to make a replica Star, going even further by rebuilding it as 4-4-2 No.40 *North Star* amongst many others. Around 1995 an approach was made by Pete Waterman to buy 7027 from the Trust. This raised questions again about 5043 if 7027 was sold. Agreement was finally reached with Pete to sell the bare bones of 7027 retaining common parts which could be used for the restoration of 5043. This had brought about the engine's movement from its exposed position, and it took up residence around the turntable with volunteers carrying out cleaning and protection work for the first time in quite a while.

During the period between 1995 and 1998, the works at Tyseley had been concentrating on the restoration and overhaul of 7760, 9600, and then 4965 *Rood Ashton Hall*, but the trustees had agreed during that period that 5043 would be the next loco to be rebuilt, following the results achieved with Panniers 7760 and 9600 and the almost completed 4965. One of the leading proponents of the 5043 rebuild was 18-year-old Alastair Meanley, who was leading a gang of young volunteers carrying out some remarkable work on 4965. It has to be revealed that this group had started some lead-in works on 5043 some time before formal commencement. It was obvious that the engine would have to be totally stripped for assessment and it was further resolved that every effort would be made to replicate the standard of work which would have been put into such a job at Swindon. It would become the biggest job probably ever to be carried out on a Castle in the post-BR era. With Tyseley's re-emergence on main line operations in 1998, nothing but the best would do for operations at 75mph on Railtrack lines. Up to this time, five of the surviving Castles had been put back into working order but the extent of repairs carried out to them had been limited by available resource, and it was felt that with growing competence and knowledge it would be an interesting challenge to find out just what a fully overhauled Castle was really capable of.

Work started with the removal of the boiler, followed by removal of the coupled wheels. The engine had been separated from its bogie in 1986 when that was temporarily used under 5080, whilst its own was receiving attention during the rebuild of that engine. The frames were set up on stands in the works and battle started. Obviously, they were stripped back to bare metal all over and checked for fractures and excessive corrosion. The very rusty dragbox was removed as was all of the platform plating and the cab side panels. The cylinders were cleaned out and valve chests re-bored. The cylinders were found to be in remarkably good order and did not require re-boring, mainly thanks to Jim's patent mixture. All cylinder cover and valve chest studs were replaced, particularly because certain of the cylinder studs also act as stays in the steam port area and can be prone to fracture. Removal of the coupled wheels presented a little more difficulty than usual as several of the axleboxes were jammed in the horns and required to be jacked down out of the frames. The frames were surveyed using our recently produced gauging gear and we found some interesting results which indicated that at its last repair, the horns had probably been ground by hand rather than by Swindon's unique horn grinding machine. Luckily, we had recently completed our own horn grinding machine and it was brought to bear on the somewhat misaligned horns. The coupled wheel tyres were turned back to profile and the journals were dealt with at the same time. Axleboxes had their bronze horn liners renewed, and re-machined to be a close fit in the newly ground horn blocks. The white metal linings of the axlebox crown brasses were renewed and turned to the new journal sizes. One obstacle which presented itself was the condition of the crank pins in the built up crank axle. These are notoriously difficult to recondition and whilst there are companies with equipment which will do the job, their charges were at the time considered to be prohibitive. By great good fortune, we were able to locate an original old fashioned journal scraper of the type which might have been in use 100 years ago. After a little re-conditioning and the manufacture of a new scraper blade for the correct crankpin profile, all that was needed was a lot of energy and around 60 hours of the author's 2004 Christmas holiday to bring the crank pins back to sparkling condition well within the tight tolerances for ovality and taper laid down by Swindon. This avoided expenditure of many thousands of pounds which was needed elsewhere within the project. All of the coupled wheel springs, spring bolts, tee link pins and rubber auxiliary spring pads were renewed before the wheels were refitted to the frame.

The absence of main rods has already been noted. Luckily, we had to hand the set of Castle motion which local enthusiast Gerald Cattell had acquired for his private museum. This included the inside and outside connecting rods. The outside rods, according to stampings, appear to have originated on 5000 *Launceston Castle*, before migrating to 5011 *Tintagel Castle* in later times. They are to the early pattern with clip on oil boxes for the small end lubrication. On the engine's visit to Euston station in 2011, it was interesting to observe that whilst 5043 had never before been to Euston, the connecting rods had been there some 84 years earlier when fitted to 5000. On the piston valve front, new valve heads, valve rings and all sleeves and gland rings were made, together with several valve chest covers for which a new casting pattern was required. We were in possession of the pistons and crossheads for the engine, but, sadly, the outside piston rods had been cut through in the scrapyard. We therefore substituted the outside pistons, rods and matching crossheads from 7027 and were able to turn the pistons down to the required size as they were slightly too large for 5043's current cylinder size. On starting the project, we were fortunate to be able to acquire quite a number of original valve motion parts from other organisations, whilst items from the Tyseley stores made up many of the deficiencies. A number of motion pins were renewed, otherwise original items were flaw tested and reground. All of the bronze motion bushes were renewed. The substantial bearings supporting the expansion links were re-metalled and machined to size. The expansion link paths were re-ground and new die blocks made to fit. The reversing shaft and auxiliary reversing shaft bearings were also renewed as wear in these manifests itself as knock in the cab reverser which can be extremely tedious to a crew subjected to it for several hours. As an aside; a considerable number of man hours were expended in polishing away the years of neglect for the motion and bringing it back to as new appearance. This was particularly so with the outside crossheads and slidebars which were not normally polished, but which were so done to replicate the polished crossheads on 4073 and 4003 as preserved. It is also worth noting that both the outside crossheads and slidebars were rarely polished in service, all but the working surfaces were painted black and polished slidebars on Castles are sadly a myth perpetrated by the preservation movement. We are guilty as charged.

The brake system was given particular attention with every pin, bolt and bush renewed. We actually collected all the parts together before commencing assembly and it was quite amazing just how many parts there were. The air pump was completely overhauled and fitted with new valves, and a new vacuum retaining valve was made and fitted. We fortunately had one of the 30 inch diameter brake cylinders to hand and that was overhauled and fitted with a new sliding band. What pipework we had was pickled and passivated to remove internal rust and scale from the inside of the pipes and much new pipework was added to complete the system.

We were fortunate to have a mechanical lubricator in the stores as it was nearly given away to another project by a previous engineering management. It was stripped down to its component parts. All of the small ball valves and springs were replaced as were various seals. New lubricator atomisers were needed. Fortunately, Swindon used Standard LMS items, presumably because they had patterns available following the construction of LMS 8F 2-8-0s during the Second World War. Patterns were available, and the check and test valves fitted to the atomisers were manufactured in-house from castings made using our own patterns. It was at this point that something of a puzzle arose regarding the actual arrangement of the lubricator pipework situated under the front right hand corner of the engine platform. Whilst a drawing was available, it quickly became obvious that it was only a general indication, produced to preserve the honour of the drawing office as the tangle of pipes was far too complex for anyone to stand a chance of producing a totally accurate drawing and it was almost certainly left for the coppersmiths to carry on doing their own thing along the lines of the drawing, which in all probability was produced after the first fitment anyway! Alastair undertook the fabrication and fitting of all of this pipework and many days later had produced something of a masterpiece of pipe fitting.

The bogie was still separated from the frame and it was comprehensively stripped, with many of the frame bolts being renewed with items made from steel to the same high strength requirements of the originals. The bogie centre slides were overhauled and the side control springs were tested to ensure that they still retained the correct load values. The wheel tyres were turned as were the axle journals and the white metal bearing surfaces of the axleboxes were completely renewed and machined to comply with Swindon standards for bearing clearances. Four new axlebox underkeeps were required as the originals were missing. These are rather complex affairs with completely enclosed oil wells and felt pads for applying the oil to axle journals. The patterns for casting them in gunmetal are similarly complicated and the whole job is not a particular favourite at the foundry, but needs must! Both bogie bearing springs were renewed, with work also required to the spring bolts and trunnions in the equalising beams. The beam rubbing strips in the axle box tops were also renewed. One issue which has arisen on several of the Castles which we have dealt with are the bolts securing the bolster casting to the engine frame. We have come across quite a number of fractured bolts, indeed one extracted from 5029 fell in half when dropped on the floor after removal, so these are now renewed as a matter of course.

The platform plates along the side of the engine are generally considered by many to be little more than a walkway but they do have a more serious function because they provide lateral stiffness to the main frame plates. It is not unusual to find loose rivets and even cracking in such plates and in the case of 5043 they were by now very heavily corroded so the whole lot came off and went to the scrap bin. At the same time, what was left of the splashers was also sent to the bin and new ones fabricated including the one for the combined left driving and trailing splashers which is actually a somewhat complicated fabrication also containing the fire iron tunnel. It was interesting to note that the original still contained the very heavily corroded remnants of a reporting number panel used in the well-known GWR reporting number frame. New splasher beading was produced for us by Swindon trained coppersmith Trevor Tremblen, so something of the new originated in Swindon. To complete the new splashers, new nameplates were required as one original was in Swindon museum and the other was at York. To aid the process, NRM curator Jim Rees offered to produce a brass rubbing of the plate to enable correct positioning of all the letters. Jim provided a short visitor entertainment, perched on a ladder carrying out the operation, as the plate was on a wall about fifteen feet above the floor. Due to the heavily corroded condition of what remained of the cab, almost the entire structure was renewed. Some subtle changes were made to the roof profile to bring it within the Network Rail height requirements whilst retaining something of the original's characteristic shape. We did re-use the original pressed steel cab side stiffeners, which are so necessary to enable the cab sides to support the heavy overhang of the extended cab roof. The steel cab floor plates were replaced as was its support structure. Once reassembled, new wooden floorboards were fitted. Rather than using softwood we now use either Keruing or more often Sapele. Whilst more expensive, we have found the woods to be unbelievably durable and long lasting just so long as you can stop the careless dropping of live fire on them during disposal. The original Swindon painting schedules specify handrails to be bare metal. In service they quickly blackened due to oily hands, but we decided to use stainless steel bar for them so that they would remain bright without us having to carry out endless scouring to keep them so. None of the original cab windows had survived to be rescued from Barry, so side and weather board window frames all had to be made and furnished with new rubber seals and 6mm laminated glass. It is often not immediately obvious that Castles and Kings were fitted with hand operated window wipers to the front windows, and we were fortunate to have obtained some time ago the original Swindon patterns for these, so just another fitment that needed casting, machining and fitting, and in fact all of our tender engines including 4965 *Rood Ashton Hall* are now so equipped. Finally, a very small original feature which required renewal was the 1950s spring loaded clips for retaining the plastic drivers' name labels which were issued for a short while during that era; they of course then required a batch of driver's nameplates for all of the usual characters whom we had driving and firing them.

The boiler had remarkably survived a lengthy period of neglect. It was built as an HC type, new in March 1955 and originally fitted to 5036, between March 1955 and April 1957. It was then fitted to 5073 between September 1957 and June 1959, and 7034 between November 1959 and October 1961. Interestingly, 7034 was turned off its final HG repair in late 1961 fitted with the last brand new spare boiler constructed at Swindon a short time before. It will be deduced from these short spans between boiler overhaul, that they were considerable contributors to the expense of maintaining steam locos in front line service. From the examination of various engine and boiler record cards it is evident that the average period which a Castle would retain a boiler was around two years. It seems that following a heavy repair with the renewal of the inner copper firebox, a boiler would undergo a couple of intermediate repairs where tubes and a number of firebox side stays were replaced, but after its third period in use, a boiler could expect to have a considerable amount of work undertaken amounting to complete renewal of the inner firebox, new three-quarter in. steel firebox sides and steel backplate as well as all tubes and stays. This was doubtless not a cheap activity but seems to be the method by which the Western Region avoided the necessity of changing large numbers of stays and tubes on depots which other BR regions practiced to keep their boilers in traffic for longer periods; there appears to be little remaining evidence of any economic assessment of this approach.

Repairs required to 5043's boiler mainly concerned the building up of discrete areas of wastage, renewal of all tubes, superheater flues and elements, renewal of all steel and a number of copper firebox side stays, renewal of the lower firebox wrapper plate and throatplate, replacement of all foundation ring rivets, together with a number of inner firebox flange rivets, renewal of the smokebox tubeplate and first barrel ring dry extension piece, the fitting of new top feed trays, re-facing of all boiler mounting pads and faces and the complete replacement of all studs, washout plugs and boiler hand hole doors and bridges. The smokebox had survived quite well, save for a gas cut hole where someone had helped themselves to a steam pipe in Barry without dismantling it properly. A lot of that sort of thing happened at

Barry where the thoughtless cut holes in boiler plates to remove washout doors rather than undo them, causing huge potential repair costs for anyone buying the loco later. The smokebox was basically overhauled and the smokebox door re-seated, but the external pitting was something of a challenge to the painters. It will probably see out another ten year boiler period but will by then be near the end of its days as a smokebox! A new hinged smokebox door crossbar and brackets was manufactured and installed. One major item of expense in the smokebox was the renewal of the main steam pipes. The engines fitted with four row boilers had an arrangement of main steam pipes which was quite different to the original arrangement, and indeed different to that of the Kings in that the enlarged superheater header had four pipes connected to it, one for each cylinder, although the inside cylinder pipes joined with each other at a tee piece connecting them to the inside cylinder casting. They are not a straightforward piece of pipe bending and sadly the number of companies capable of such work continue to diminish. Production of such items requires a little extra (known as green ends) to be left on the pipes to allow for final trimming on the job and that has to be very carefully carried out to ensure that too much is not cut off and the pipes left short. They then require the specially machined end with their joint faces to be welded to them, not forgetting to slip on their loose flanges before doing so. Joint faces to the pipes are metal to metal with no gaskets or other joint materials but there are other joints, especially those to the cylinders, which originally used heavy section corrugated copper joints known as Hulberd rings. It is no surprise to know that they are no longer available and have become just another item which has to be manufactured in house from machined copper rings.

Of course, other pipework exists within the smokebox, much of it copper and that has a very hard life, quite often requiring renewal in service due to attrition. The most essential is probably that to the blower which can effectively cripple the engine should it burst, but worst is the supply to the steam lance cock which carries live steam at all times meaning that should it burst there is considerable danger of a blow back into the cab. Finally, and prior to refitting the completed and tested boiler to the frame, it required a new ashpan. Unlike many of the high superheat Castles, 5043 had retained the original style of a two part ashpan fitted with four damper doors, and we decided to manufacture the new ashpan to the original design rather than the later hopper arrangement which would need further work to produce all of the operating gear. As with all our engines, the ashpan was fitted with flushing pipes supplied by a connection to the injector delivery pipes. This enables both damping down the ash contents and also a means of fire suppression when working on the main line. Damping down the ash is most useful when disposing the engine as it almost completely eliminates the clouds of ash which can occur adding to the task of maintaining the cleanliness of the engine. All damper doors are additionally fitted with fixed spark screens to prevent any live fire from dropping out of the ashpan, as many fires can be caused by emissions from the ashpan rather than just the chimney. The last modification to the ashpan was the addition of bottom doors of the butterfly pattern which considerably aid ash disposal. The doors are of a remarkably simple and economical pattern and are very much based on a similar arrangement fitted to the LMS Royal Scots in the early 1950s.

One important modern requirement is the subject of spark arresting. This is because far less care is expended on controlling lineside vegetation than was the case back in the steam era. Lineside fires are treated far more seriously than was the case then, and it is possible for serious damage to be caused to lineside signal and telecoms cabling which can often be laid on the ground or in the lineside cess area. The fire brigade will also require the line to be closed until all traces of the fire are extinguished. Network Rail will be extremely concerned about the amount of delay caused to other services and the consequent delay attribution cost can be eye watering. For all these reasons, spark arresting has become a subject to be seriously studied. We originally fitted a new basket arrestor of the original pattern fitted in the 1950s to 5043 and initial trials indicated that it did indeed arrest sparks. The only trouble was that it did it too well and a journey from Birmingham to York would fill the smokebox with char to a level half way from the door crossbar to the top of the smokebox door ring, and that started to cause problems. We therefore started to look at the self-cleaning smokebox arrangement which was fitted to the Kings in the early 1950s. A similar arrangement was also fitted to 7018 when it became the first double chimney Castle, but sadly no drawings of that arrangement are known to exist, so it was back to first principles and the King arrangement as something of a guide. Fortunately, both the superheater header and the blast pipe still carry some cast mounting points which acted as a guide as well. We were able to construct a suitable arrangement which gave encouraging indications when put into use, but it did require several modifications to optimise it. First of all, we tried several different sizes and patterns of mesh until one was found which would break up particles, control the size of emissions and importantly not allow particles to become wedged in it, clogging the mesh and impairing steaming. We soon discovered that in the limited space in front of the screen (Castle smokeboxes can be pretty crowded even before fitting spark arrestors) the horizontal smokebox door crossbar was restricting the gas flow and thereby accelerating it, causing large quantities of particles to be wedged in the mesh and obstructing it. The answer lay in the vertical cross bar which was fitted in many BR standard engines and that particular problem then went away once we had made and fitted such an item. The self-cleaning gear depends on a certain amount of turbulence in the area immediately behind the smokebox door to circulate the particles of char, etc., until they are effectively broken down to a size which will pass through the mesh. To assist this process, a vane is attached at the front and below the table plate, and an adjustable vane was made and fitted, being adjusted a number of times until a satisfactory size and angle of attack were established. This gear now performs in a highly satisfactory manner without any of the restrictions on performance which many experts predict, the many outstanding performances of the engine serve to confirm its efficiency.

Once the boiler had been returned to the frames, attention was turned to making and fitting the new boiler cleating. The sheets fitted to the boiler barrel and firebox sides were CNC cut using a programme which is able to determine the exact true shape of the tapered cleating. Boiler insulation consists of heavyweight blown ceramic fibre matting rather than the asbestos fibre plaster originally used. The modern material performs very efficiently and has proven to noticeably reduce fuel consumption over time.

At the time of recovery from Barry scrapyard, all the bronze boiler mountings and copper pipework had long since disappeared into the melting pot, and there was no alternative but to completely recreate them from scratch. At Tyseley we are fortunate to possess casting patterns for just about any of the common GWR boiler mountings, so this situation presents few problems other than that of finding the necessary cash! Consequently, almost all of the boiler mounting were newly made with a few minor exceptions such as the three way lubricator cock on the manifold where a number of new spare items exist in the stores. The whistles are also originals, one having been retrieved from a King in Cashmore's scrapyard. The re-establishment of all of the pipework was also a matter destined to further drain the coffers. Whilst some of the injector steam and delivery pipes are formed from steel tube, there is a considerable quantity of copper pipe of larger bore to find as well as a fair amount of the smaller copper pipes for smaller steam and vacuum services. One particular problem solved in house was a rather complex and tightly bent section of 4 inch copper pipe from the exhaust steam pipe to the exhaust injector. Fortunately, we had a length of the correct sized pipe in stock and the said pipe was bent in house, with not a little pride in its successful manufacture. The exhaust injector was a stroke of luck as there is a distinct shortage of genuine exhaust injectors. Until recently, no patterns have existed and most restorers have opted to replace them with a live steam injector as the complication of exhaust injector maintenance is not really necessary for preserved line use. That is further underlined by a widespread lack of understanding of the really quite simple method of operating them and it is truly remarkable to see the mess which some latter day firemen get into trying to operate them. We were fortunate to be able to broker a deal for replacing an exhaust injector with a live steam one and we were quite happy to provide and fit a new live steam injector and modify the pipework to suit in exchange for the exhaust injector. After overhaul and return to service, it has performed faultlessly, although they do have a propensity to eat the hardened stainless steel delivery cone tips at a fair rate!

The foregoing represents a very considerable amount of both work and expense and yet there was still more to do in fitting the necessary electronic systems to the engine to enable it to be run on the national network. The first requisite was a speedometer. Fortunately, we had a spare BTH speedometer generator and brackets in the stores, but we did not possess the special BTH speedometer gauge which went with it. Fortune took a hand when one of our volunteers walked into the office carrying a bag which an old friend had asked him to deliver to me. Inside was not just any old BTH gauge, but one marked with the magic letters GWR, specifically for fitting to 5043. Next on the list was the fitting of the combined automatic warning system (AWS) and the recently introduced Train Protection and Warning system (TPWS). We had by then had quite a lot of experience in the fitment of these systems, having been amongst the pioneers of its fitting to steam locomotives at the very inception of TPWS. The other necessary equipment was the data recorder, formally known as On Train Monitoring and Recording (OTMR). Here again we were well acquainted with the proprietor of one of the leading equipment manufacturers and were privileged to be able to head up a scheme which supplied over sixty sets of equipment to various loco owners to enable them to fit the equipment themselves with considerable cost savings. The fitting of all this equipment to 5043 had by now just become a routine job and proceeded with little difficulty.

All this really only left one matter requiring resolution – the tender. Or rather, the lack of a tender! We did have a rather woebegone tender frame around the yard. We had scrapped the badly corroded tank some time before. The origins of it were uncertain but it is likely that it had seen service with a King in the early 1950s as deep down in the layers of paint it had been blue at one time. We had decided some time before that we would very much like to have a flat sided Hawksworth tender and early on in the programme I had drawn up a replacement Hawksworth tank with the intent of putting it on the Collett frame. That was not as crazy as it sounds, because some detailed consideration of the drawings revealed that the actual arrangement of positioning the tank on the frames was exactly the same, rather raising the question if that had formed an intention of using the welded Hawksworth tank for future replacement of corroded Collett tanks. Sadly, we shall never find an answer to that but it is definitely possible to do. Not long after, an opportunity arose for a bulk buying deal and we found ourselves with a new Hawksworth type tender tank. Soon after we were able to acquire a spare Hawksworth frame. The Hawksworth tenders were fitted with standard wheelsets, axles, axleboxes, brake gear, buffing and drawgear; all of which we possessed on the spare Collett frames. That meant that we effectively had all of the major components to build our very own Hawksworth 4,000. gallon tender, otherwise officially described as '4,000 gallons flush bottom tender with welded tank'. We did of course have to produce quite a number of minor parts for the tender, as well as the pipework and its brackets for the vacuum and steam heating and a new vacuum reservoir. Due to the difference between the two types of tender, we did have to manufacture a new handbrake column and shaft, as well as fitting our own design of operating gear for the feed water cocks having deemed the original pattern on the Hawksworth tenders to be too complicated. The wheelsets had their tyres and journals turned and new axlebox bearing brasses were made and fitted, as were axlebox oil pads. The bearing springs and rubber auxiliaries were all renewed as well. We produced the usual mass of bushes, pins and bolts for the brake gear, and overhauled the tender brake cylinder. Provision was made for the now very necessary low level water fillers which allow tenders to be refilled whilst standing under overhead electric line equipment.

As the task came to its conclusion, the last remaining job was to deal with all the paperwork leading to acceptance of the locomotive to re-enter service on the national network. We shall, in the interests of brevity, just say that it was an interesting task and move on, as it would perhaps generate a further chapter. All that then remained was to try it out and run some acceptance trials. One or two issues did surface, but on the whole its passage into service was remarkably fault free, and just serves to demonstrate what incredibly good locomotives they actually are. All you have to do is mend them properly, maintain them carefully, and use them sensibly and they will just simply perform. Of course nobody ever promised that all of that would be easy. And it is certainly no longer cheap. We never really counted but we did reckon that if it had been a truly commercial job at the then commercial rates, it would probably have cost £1.4 million at 2008 prices. Given recent circumstances and inflation relating to materials needed, that would be a lot more at 2021 prices. But it might still be considered a bargain when one hears of the costs of other restorations, and we started with the absolute bare bones of an engine!

5043 at the Barry scrapyard of Dai Woodham, 9 June 1967. (Brian Penney)

Above left: **5043's smokebox** and boiler sit removed from the frames at Tyseley, April 2000. (Tyseley Works)

Above right: **5043's firebox** after removal of the lower side. (Bob Meanley)

5043's completed frames ready for fitting of the boiler, 2007. (Bob Meanley)

Above left: **The new** boiler tubeplate for 5043. (Bob Meanley)

Above right: **The new** copper exhaust steam pipe made at Tyseley for 5043. (Bob Meanley)

The first steaming of 5043's boiler, 2007. The Tyseley team from left to right – Nicky Morant, Paul Brewer, Unidentified, Duncan Ballard, Alastair Meanley, John Glaze (boiler inspector) and Bob Meanley. (Bob Meanley Collection)

5043's boiler is lifted into its frames at Tyseley, October 2007. (Bob Meanley)

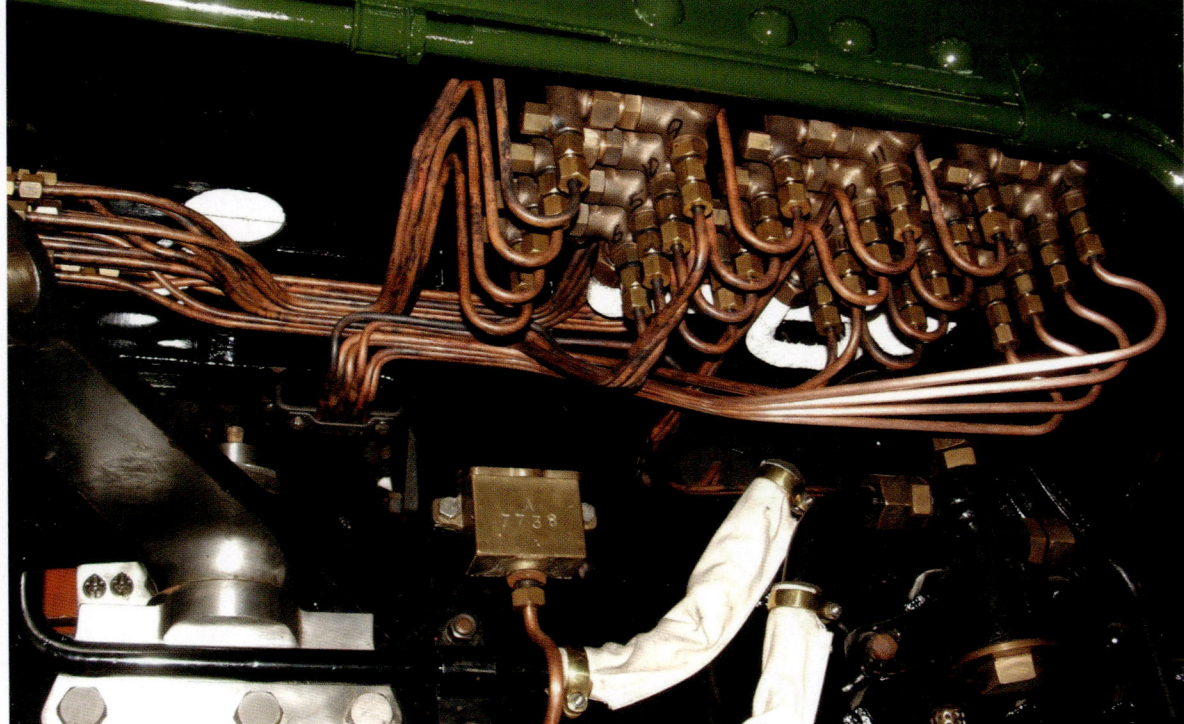

Above left: **5043's smokebox** showing the new pipework. (Bob Meanley)

Above right: **New wire** mesh self-cleaning screens are installed later, after experience in traffic. (Bob Meanley)

Left: **The completed** oil pipework fabricated and installed by Alastair Meanley for the mechanical lubrication system of 5043. (Bob Meanley)

Above: **The completed** nameplate with the name 'Earl of Mount Edgcumbe' carefully copied from the original nameplate exhibited in the NRM at York. The second original nameplate is at STEAM Museum at Swindon. (Bob Meanley)

Right: **The driver's** side of 5043's cab. (Bob Meanley)

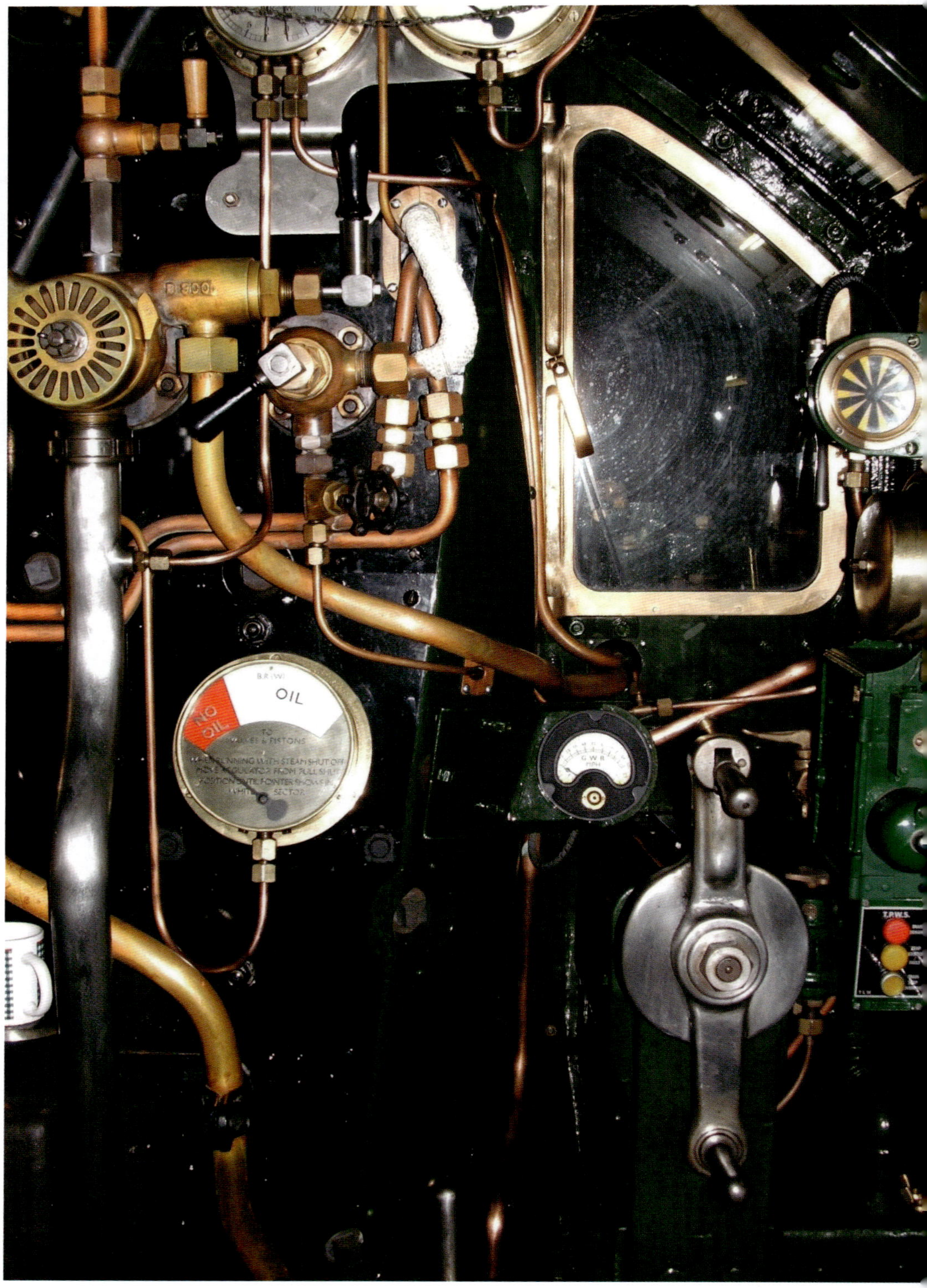

Operation (by David Maidment)
In the summer of 2009 5043 took over the regular running of the *Shakespeare Express* from the more usual 4965 and showed what it could do with sprints over the last stretch of the main line back from Hatton, passed at around 25mph, to the Tyseley stop, averaging over 60mph for the 13.34 miles, pass-to-stop. I show a couple of runs made on the same day with the return lunchtime and afternoon trains.

The Shakespeare Express

5043 *Earl of Mount Edgcumbe*

8 chs, 277/295 tons

Driver Churchill

Firemen Bob Meanley (trip 1) Alastair Meanley (trip 2)

Miles	Location	Times	Speeds		Times	Speeds	
0	Hatton North Junction	00.00	26*	3 L	00.00	24½ *	T
3.60	Lapworth	04.10	70		04.16	68½	
6.24	Dorridge	06.18	73/72		06.26	71½ /71	
6.72	Bentley Crossing	06.48	73		06.56	72½	
8.15	Widney Manor	07.49	76½		07.58	77½	
9.54	Solihull	08.59	77		09.07	78	
11.4	Olton	10.25	78/75		10.30	78	
12.37	Acocks Green	11.13	68½		11.16	68½	
13.34	Tyseley	13.02		1 E	12.59		4 E

In the late Spring of 2009, 5043 was rostered to a run over Shap just a couple of weeks after the preserved 46115 *Scots Guardsman* had shown its mastery of the gradients. There was some anxiety in the minds of GW enthusiasts as previous runs with 5029 *Nunney Castle* and 6024 *King Edward I* over Shap had both had problems and the 1967 successful assault with 7029 *Clun Castle* had only seven coaches. They need not have worried for 5043 and its crew restored the pride of the GWR.

Carlisle-Crewe via Settle & Carlisle, 20 June 2009

1Z80 7.08am Tyseley/Crewe-Carlisle

5043 *Earl of Mount Edgcumbe* –Tyseley

10chs, 351/383 tons

Driver Bill Andrew, Fireman Alastair Meanley

Miles	Location	Times	Speeds	Gradients
0	Crewe	00.00	2 L	
	Coal Yard	03.29	29	
	MP 163	08.43	63	L

		Carlisle-Crewe via Settle & Carlisle, 20 June 2009		
		1Z80 7.08am Tyseley/Crewe-Carlisle		
		5043 *Earl of Mount Edgcumbe* –Tyseley		
		10chs, 351/383 tons		
		Driver Bill Andrew, Fireman Alastair Meanley		
Miles	Location	Times	Speeds	Gradients
8.7	Winsford	10.55	73/77½	1/300 F
	Hartford	14.19	75/72	1/360 R
14.4	Acton Bridge	16.33	76	1/330 F
16.2	Weaver Junction	18.25	pws 40* 2 E	
21.2	Moore	23.18	73	1/180 F, 1/567 F
24	Warrington	26.03	64*/69 2 E	
	Winwick Junction	29.02	71	
29.8	Golborne Junction	31.11	67½	1/156 R
33.2	Bamfurlong	33.59	75	1/417 F
	Springs Branch Jcn	35.01	71 3 E	L
35.8	Wigan	36.12	69	
38	Boar's Head	38.09	61½	1/104 R
41.6	Coppull Hall	40.44	63/55*	1/119 R
	Balshaw Lane	43.55/44.13 sig stand		
45.5	Euxton Junction	48.44	50	L
	Leyland	50.13	67	
50.9	Preston	56.06	8* 4 E	
	Oxhey	60.06	40	1/101 R, 1/503 R
55.7	Barton	64.17	63	L
	Brock	66.41	75	1/644 F
60.4	Garstang	-	76	L
	Bay Horse	72.55	75	L
	Oubeck	75.06	76/70	
71.9	Lancaster	80.41	sigs 13*/ 30/ sigs 13* 2 ½ E	
	Morecambe Junction	85.20	53	
75	Hest Bank	86.31	60	L
	Bolton-le-Sands	-	sigs 11*	

Carlisle-Crewe via Settle & Carlisle, 20 June 2009

1Z80 7.08am Tyseley/Crewe-Carlisle

5043 *Earl of Mount Edgcumbe* –Tyseley

10chs, 351/383 tons

Driver Bill Andrew, Fireman Alastair Meanley

Miles	Location	Times	Speeds		Gradients
78.2	Carnforth Gds Loop	92.36		1 E	(water & pathing stop)
		00.00		2 L	
0	Carnforth	01.26	25		
	MP 9½	06.21	42		1/134 R
4.5	Burton	07.48	60		L
7.3	Milnthorpe	10.20	67½		1/173 R
	Hincaster Junction	12.11	64		1/173 R
12.8	Oxenholme	15.45	58	2 E	1/111 R, 1/178 R
	Lambrigg Crossing	-	52	2/3rd reg, 28% cut-off	1/131 R, 1/106 R
19.9	Grayrigg	23.47	46		1/106 R
	Dillicar	27.44	72		L
25.9	Tebay	29.18	78	6 E	1/146 R
	MP 35	32.00	55		1/75 R
28.9	Scout Green	-	48	2/3rd reg, 33% cut-off	1/75 R
	MP 37½	35.17	40		1/75 R
31.4	Shap summit	35.33	44½		1/75 R, L
	Shap	37.45	65		
	MP 41½	42.09/45.45 sig stand (track inspection – flood)			
	Thrimby Grange	49.47	56		1/125 F
40.7	Clifton	53.20	74		1/125 F
44.9	Penrith	56.55	67	2 L	
	Plumpton	60.53	75		1/186 F, L
55.4	Southwaite	65.46	68/73		1/228 F
57.9	Wreay	68.00	66		1/184 F
	Upperby Bridge	71.08	72/50*		1/131 F
62.8	Carlisle	75.47		¾ L	

Miles	Location	Times	Speeds	Schedule	Gradients
		1Z84 4.11pm Carlisle-Tyseley, 20 June 2009			
		5043 *Earl of Mount Edgcumbe* –Tyseley			
		10 chs, 351/380 tons			
0	Carlisle	00.00		1 L	
	Upperby Junction	03.08	30		
4.9	Wreay	09.50	41		1/131 R
7.4	Southwaite	13.04	52		1/228 R
13.1	Plumpton	19.13	56/67		1/164 R, L
	MP 54	21.03	64		1/186 R
17.9	Penrith	23.27	72	1½ E	
	Eden Valley Jcn	26.09	74/70		1/191 F, 1/193 R
22.2	Clifton	27.03	66		1/125 R
	Thrimby Grange	31.06	55/ 53½		1/125 R
29.5	Shap	34.48	57		1/142 R, L
31.5	Shap summit	37.05	54		1/106 R
34	Scout Green	-	76/72*		1/75 F
37	Tebay	41.51	77/70*	7 E	1/146 F
	Dillicar	43.36	69		L
	Low Gill	45.21	73		L
43.1	Grayrigg	47.03	65		
	Lambrigg Crossing	-	74/71*		1/131 F
50	Oxenholme	52.48	75	9 E	1/178 F
	Sedgwick	54.32	78/74*		1/111 F
53.6	Hincaster Junction	55.47	70		1/193 F
55.5	Milnthorpe	57.28	70		1/173 F
	MP 9½	61.05	67/57		
	MP 6 ½	67.48/77.35 sig stand		11 E	
62.8	Carnforth Gds Loop	81.49 (70 net)		1 L	

The year 2010 was the 175th anniversary of the Great Western Railway and during a chance conversation between Matthew Golton, Projects Director for First Great Western, and Bob Meanley, Matthew queried what the preservation industry intended to do to celebrate it. It was suggested that a re-run of the train which was instituted by the GWR in 1935 to celebrate its Centenary in 1935 might be appropriate, and consequently the idea of running a nonstop *Bristolian* for the first time in fifty-one years was born. The notion was taken forward at a joint meeting between Network Rail, West Coast Railways, First Great Western (as it then was), and Tyseley, held at Euston station of all places, and agreement was reached that it would be examined in detail, and in due course the subsequent plan was put into action. This train became one of the principal attractions of a programme of events developed by various GWR focused heritage organisations, which also opted to involve the 'Railway Children' charity as a beneficiary of fund-raising activity. The detailed planning between the four parties proceeded apace, and one of the major obstacles was of course concern over water capacity. After much consideration, a GUV was converted to provide the additional water required to avoid the need for a water stop. The final plan envisaged two railtours involving one set of customers running up to London in an HST special and returning on the morning Down *Bristolian* and another set of passengers riding down to Bristol in the HST and returning with the Up *Bristolian*. David Maidment and a team of volunteers conducted a raffle on both trains and raised over £1,000 for the charity. Footplate crew for the day were Inspector Andy Taylor, Driver Ray Poole and Firemen Alastair and Bob Meanley. The Down journey was completed nonstop after successfully negotiating its path around other services, but the return run was more special, thanks to good fortune combining with the efforts of FGW and Network Rail staff who managed to somehow clear the road and allow the *Bristolian* to live up to its name.

The Bristolian, Bristol to Paddington via Badminton [GW 175]
Saturday 17 April 2010
5043 *Earl of Mount Edgcumbe* 84E
8 chs, 300/315 tons
Driver Andy Taylor, Firemen Alastair & Bob Meanley

Miles	Location	Times	Speeds	Schedule
0	Bristol Temple Meads	00.00		T
	Dr Days Junction	02.50	26	¼ E
1.6	Stapleton Road	04.33	40	
	Narroways Hill Jcn	05.12	36	¾ E
2.5	Horfield	-	27	
4.8	Filton Junction	10.09	31/ sigs 13*	T
6.2	Bristol Parkway	13.50	36	¾ L
	MP 110	16.04	56	
	Westerleigh Junction	18.57	63	T
13	Sodbury Tunnel	22.14	67	
17.6	Badminton	25.37	62	
23.4	Hullavington	30.28	78/80	6E
27.9	Little Somerford	33.54	78	
	MP 87	-	75	
34.7	Wootton Bassett	39.21	66*	8½ E
40.3	Swindon	44.17	74/72	11¾ E
	MP 75	-	77	
46	Shrivenham	48.48	77	

		The Bristolian, Bristol to Paddington via Badminton [GW 175]		
		Saturday 17 April 2010		
		5043 *Earl of Mount Edgcumbe* 84E		
		8 chs, 300/315 tons		
		Driver Andy Taylor, Firemen Alastair & Bob Meanley		
Miles	**Location**	**Times**	**Speeds**	**Schedule**
51.1	Uffington	52.44	78	14¾ E
53.7	Challow	54.39	80/78	15½ E
57.2	Wantage Road	57.30	78	19½ E
61.1	Steventon	60.54	sigs 64*/70	
64.5	Didcot	63.33	78	20½ E
69.2	Cholsey	67.08	78	
72.9	Goring	70.00	75	
76.1	Pangbourne	72.34	77/78	
79	Tilehurst	74.48	75	
	Scours Lane	-	sigs 41*	
81.6	Reading	77.43	49	25¼ E
	Sonning	-	66	
86.6	Twyford	82.26	74	25½ E
	Ruscombe Sidings	-	78/80	
93.4	Maidenhead	87.41	79	28¼ E
	Taplow	89.03	76	
	Burnham	90.15	77	
99.1	Slough	92.13	77	30¾ E
	Langley	93.59	74	
	Iver	95.10	76	
104.4	West Drayton	96.22	77	
	Heathrow Airport Jcn	98.00	73	33 E
	Hayes	98.14	73	
108.5	Southall	99.42	76	35¼ E
	Hanwell	-	76	
	West Ealing	101.41	75	37¼ E
111.9	Ealing Broadway	102.23	74	
113.3	Acton	103.35	73	39 E
	Ladbroke Grove	105.48	42*	40¼ E
<u>117.6</u>	<u>Paddington</u>	<u>109.58</u>	[106 mins net]	<u>44 E</u>

Report from Bob Meanley on footplate: 5043 worked with 2nd valve of regulator just cracked and 15 per cent cut-off. Increasing cut-off to 17 per cent produced acceleration to over 75-80mph and engine brought back to 15 per cent. In fact, surprisingly, the use of the GUV water carrier proved unnecessary. 5043 completed the 118 mile run on 2,700 gallons of water (22.9 gallons per mile) and 2 tons of coal (37.3lbs per mile).

A year later, 5043 was again rostered for a visit to the Northern Fells, with a railtour named *The Pride of Swindon*. The log of the return from Carlisle to Hellifield is shown below together with an excerpt of a run a couple of years later when 5043 had been paired with 6201 *Princess Elizabeth* on the northbound run via Shap but had to take the load via the Settle & Carlisle southbound unassisted as 6201 failed at Carlisle with a hot tender axlebox. The Appleby (start) – Ais Gill summit (pass) time is a record for any steam train of this weight.

Carlisle-Crewe/Tyseley,

		16 October 2010			10 March 2012			
		5043 *Earl of Mount Edgcumbe*			5043			
		10 coaches + 47.773 trailing 470/503t			11chs, 387/425 tons			
		Driver Mick Kelly			Driver Gordon Hodgson			
		Fireman Alastair Meanley			Fireman Alastair Meanley			
Miles	Location	Times	Speeds		Times	Speeds		Gradients
0	Carlisle	00.00		4½ L	00.00		T	
	London Road Jcn	02.27		1 L				
0.9	Petterill Bridge Jcn	03.10	blowing off	1 L				
2.7	Scotby	08.27	32					1/132 R
3.9	Cumwhinton	10.41	38					1/132 R
	Howes Sidings	12.21	40/43	1 L				L, 1/132 R
6.8	Cotehill	-	43 blowing off					1/132 R
8.1	MP 300	-	42					1/132 R
10	Armathwaite	19.22	53					
	Barton Wood	-	59/57 blowing off					1/220 R
15.5	Lazonby	24.47	68	1E				1/165 F
18.4	Little Salkeld	27.39	64					1/132 R
19.8	Langwathby	29.17	57 blowing off					1/110 R
23.4	Culgaith	32.56	62	2½ E				1/330 R
24.7	New Biggin	-	57					1/132 R
27.9	Long Marston	37.37	63 blowing off					L
	MP 278	-	62/58 easy					1/120 R
30.8	Appleby	40.27		6E	43.49	(40 net)	7 E	

		Carlisle-Crewe/Tyseley, 16 October 2010 5043 *Earl of Mount Edgcumbe* 10 coaches + 47.773 trailing 470/503t Driver Mick Kelly Fireman Alastair Meanley			10 March 2012 5043 11chs, 387/425 tons Driver Gordon Hodgson Fireman Alastair Meanley			
Miles	Location	Times	Speeds		Times	Speeds		Gradients
0	Appleby	00.00 Water		13½ E	00.00		25 E	
	Ormside Viaduct	-	50/56		04.37	57		1/176 F
2.5	Ormside	05.15	53		-			1/100 R
	Helm Tunnel	-	47 blowing off					1/100 R
5.3	Griseburn	09.25	42/40		08.21	44		1/100 R
7.5	Crosby Garrett	-	42/45		11.02	57½	23 E	1/166 R, 1/200 R
	Smardale Viaduct	13.28	49/43 blowing off			56/47		1/100 R
10.7	Kirkby Stephen	16.26	41	11E	14.41	46	23¾ E	1/100 R
	Birkett Tunnel	19.30	42/41		17.20	45		1/100 R
14	Mallerstang	-	44/47 50% cut off		19.04	46/50½	24 E	1/330 R
17.5	Ais Gill	26.07	44 ½	13E	23.31	46 (pass)	24½ E	1/100 R
20.6	Garsdale	29.20	57/60	12½ E				1/165 F
23.8	Dent	32.50	63/40*					L
28.7	Blea Moor	39.25	52/60	13E				1/440 R
	Batty Moss Viaduct	-	20*					
30	Ribblehead	42.05	30* blowing off	13E				1/100 F
	Selside	-	57					1/100 F
34.8	Horton-in-Ribblesdale	-	60 easy					1/100 F
40.8	Settle	54.05	60*					1/100 F
42.7	Settle Jcn	56.14	60*/64	15E				1/100 F
	Long Preston	-	5* sigs					
		62.20/64.50 sigs stand						
46	Hellifield	67.28		11E				

I can do no better than quote the words of Mike Notley from his regular article 'Main Line' in *Steam Railway*, writing about the 2010 trip. He was riding in the cab of the trailing diesel 47 773 and confirmed that no assistance was given at any stage:

We crossed Ormside Viaduct and entered the 'Blue Riband' section at 54mph, the steam locomotive audible from the rear of the train

as it set about the 1 in 100……
'it's doing OK' became 'it's doing very well' as we met the next stretch of 1 in 100 at 49½mph and stormed up to Kirkby Stephen at a minimum of 39mph. A brief easing …… and we were now on the most difficult section, the 1 in 100 climb through the usually wet Birkett Tunnel to Milepost 264. ….. This forced another reassessment of the position and 'very well' became 'fantastically well' as we thundered along Mallerstang Edge with speed rising to 47mph. After 1½ miles of the final stretch of 1 in 100, speed had been reduced to 43mph but the Castle had one more surprise in its locker. Driver Kelly later confided that it was in such good nick at this point, as the loco was still blowing off steam, that he opened up to 50% cut off for the last mile to Ais Gill summit and began to accelerate. The grin on my face as this magnificent locomotive confounded the GWR critics once more, just as it had on Shap a year earlier, must have been off the scale and speed crept up until, as we cleared the last quarter mile of 1 in 100 at Milepost 260, it was doing 44mph with both injectors on and the safety valves feathering.

The climb from Milepost 275 to 259¾ had involved an average edhp of around 1,575. Between 266 and 261 it had been around 1,750 and for that magic ear-splitting, spine-tingling assault on the final mile, to a stunning 2,030. The Castle had become stronger as the climb went on and to be capable of upping the figure beyond 2,000 after almost 19 minutes of hard work is nothing short of incredible. That's around 69 edhp for every square foot of grate which, if translated to a 'Duchess' would be around 3,450, a figure better than the *Duchess of Abercorn's* achievements (on a test run when the highest power output by a UK steam locomotive was recorded).

This was the highest ever recorded power output for a Castle and equal to the best 'King' records. It is perhaps worth pointing out that the famed Swindon testing team never got around to carrying out full trials of a four row, double chimney Castle, so the limit of which they were capable was never formally measured.

Further excellent performances continued to be recorded establishing the reputation of this locomotive. I travelled on the *Cornishman* railtour in April 2012 when 5043 with a 9-coach 316/340 ton load sped across the Bristol-Taunton 'flats' at a steady 75-78mph and stormed Whiteball at 53mph minimum. It then roared up Dainton with the maximum load allowed for a Castle in BR days entering the tunnel at 36mph and immediately began to blow off steam. From 60 at Totnes, Tigley Box was passed at 36mph, it then fell to 31 and accelerated to 35 at Rattery Box. On the return, Newton Abbot was passed in 40¼ minutes, with 18mph at Hemerdon summit, and 31 at Dainton. Exeter to Whiteball summit took just 21 minutes (start to pass) with 61mph entering the tunnel and 85mph was reached on the descent before brakes were applied. Taunton was reached 6 minutes early, but it was delayed there waiting for an Up HST to pass, and left 12 minutes late. Another steady charge across the flat Bridgwater-Yatton section at 75-79mph took place and even with severe signal checks in from Nailsea, Bristol was reached just one minute late. The following month 5043 set off on its weekend tour of Scotland but the promising start from Crewe – 80mph by Moore troughs, 8½ minutes early into Barton loop for water – was then spoiled as a diesel was attached at the rear at Carnforth to do most of the work, because of fire risk in the spring heatwave. 55mph at Grayrigg and 56 at Shap summit cannot therefore be claimed by 5043! The Castle with 47 760 trailing behaved itself impeccably in Scotland, early everywhere and the return on the Sunday had 37 516 at the rear instead of the 47. A weird run ensued from Carlisle as 47 760 was added to the class 37 at the rear but it was not operating as it was out of fuel. 5043 and 37 516 were therefore hauling a gross weight of over 500 tons, passing Shap summit in 42 minutes at 49mph and touching 74 before Tebay, 4 minutes early. The dead class 47 was detached at Carnforth.

5043 was in charge of the *Cheltenham Flyer* railtour in May 2013, non-stop from Gloucester to Paddington with nine coaches and GUV water-carrier, 345/375 tons. The schedule was absurdly easy and 5043 made mincemeat of it arriving at Paddington 39 minutes early in 136 minutes. Highlights were 30mph at Sapperton, 78 at Purton, 80-78-80 from Uffington to Steventon, 78½ at Pangbourne on the relief line (from Didcot), back to fast line at Ruscombe, 78 at Slough, 79 at Ealing. The return ran even earlier, arriving at Gloucester 50 minutes before schedule. After a slow start out to Westbourne Park crossing there to the fast line behind an HST, 5043 accelerated to 75 by Hayes, 79 at Slough and maintained that speed passing Reading in 36½ minutes, 20 minutes early! After 30mph through Reading, 74 at Goring and then relief lines through Didcot, back to fast line at Foxhall Junction. 77mph at Shrivenham and walking pace through Swindon saw us a full half hour early there (89¾ minutes), 75 after Minety and 44 minimum at Sapperton made us 54 early at Standish Junction followed by another 75 and signals to a stand outside Gloucester station – 141¾ minutes.

The *piece de resistance* was the second Z48 Anniversary Train the day after 5029's run mentioned earlier. The Down special was hauled by class 52, D1015 *Western Champion*. The return with 5043 and 7 coaches plus the GUV water-carrier broke 7029's Plymouth-Bristol non-stop record, achieving the stretch in just 133 minutes and 3 seconds. I give the highlights in the table below.

15.05 Plymouth North Road-Oxford, 1Zulu48 Anniversary Train

5043 *Earl of Mount Edgcumbe*

7 chs + water-carrier, 285/315 tons

10.5.2014 Driver Ray Churchill, Fireman Alastair Meanley, Mechanical inspector Bob Meanley.

Miles	Location	Times	Speeds		Gradients
0	Plymouth North Rd	00.00		2 L	
1.9	Laira Junction	06.27	49/62		1/83 F
6.7	Hemerdon Box	13.08	26/17	¾ E	1/42 R
	Wrangaton	23.16	50 eased		
23.2	Totnes	36.00	30 coasting/66	2 L	1/47 F, 1/66 F
28	Dainton Tunnel	41.33	31½	1½ L	1/38 R
31.8	Newton Abbot	45.49	65/71	T	
	Dawlish	-	58/65		
	Exminster	-	78		L
52	Exeter St David's	64.23	45*	18½ E	
	Tiverton Parkway	79.56	76/69/sigs 38*	18 E	1/155 R
71.9	Whiteball Box	84.41	57		1/115 R
	Wellington	-	81/75*/80		1/80 F, 1/90 F
82.8	Taunton	92.46	79	20 E	
87.5	Cogload Junction	96.38	75/82	22½ E	L
94.3	Bridgwater	101.51	77	23½ E	L
100.6	Highbridge	106.45	77		
107.9	Uphill Junction	112.29	76	24½ E	L
110.8	Worle Junction	-	78		L
115.6	Yatton	118.31	76		L
121.7	Flax Bourton	-	72/79		1/200 R, 1/180 F
125.7	Parson Street	126.36	76/40*		
127.6	Bristol Temple Meads	133.03		32 E	

5043 at Shap, still with steam to spare after surmounting Shap summit at 44mph, 20 June 2009. (Bill Andrew Collection)

The train then spent 40 minutes awaiting an onward path, leaving 5 minutes late, and gave a brisk run to Oxford, with minimum 58 after Box Tunnel, 76/72 at Dauntsey and after an 8 minute wait at Wootton Bassett for an HST off the Badminton route to precede, 80 at Uffington where 5043 was still blowing off steam. It was 10 minutes early at Foxhall Junction, but a 10 minute wait at Didcot North Junction meant that Oxford was reached more or less on time.

5043 on arrival at Carlisle after a superb run conquering Grayrigg and Shap with a Crewe-Carlisle railtour, 20 June 2009. The Pendolino is on a Glasgow-Euston service. (David Maidment)

5043 *Earl of Mount Edgcumbe* at Salisbury after arrival with the Tyseley-Salisbury *Moonraker* railtour, 3 April 2010. (David Maidment)

5043 on the return *Moonraker* railtour in the Andover area, 3 April 2010. (Author's Collection)

5043 at Banbury on the return *Moonraker* railtour, the GUV water carrier having been attached. I rode the footplate from Banbury to Solihull at the invitation of Bob Meanley, 3 April 2010. (David Maidment)

5043 and the Down *Bristolian* departing from Paddington, fireman Alastair Meanley leaning from the cab, 17 April 2010. (Bob Meanley Collection)

5043 leaves Middlehill Tunnel, Box, with the GW 175 non-stop *Bristolian* special, 17 April 2010. (*GW Echo*)

5043 passing through Sydney Gardens, Bath, with the Down *Bristolian*, 17 April 2010. (Neville Wellings)

5043 *Earl of Mount Edgcumbe* at the head of the GW 175 *Bristolian* non-stop run to Paddington before departure from Bristol Temple Meads, 17 April 2010. (David Maidment)

5043 Earl of Mount Edgcumbe • 107

5043 on arrival at Bristol Temple Meads with the *Bristolian* special, 17 April 2010. Note the BR GUV water carrier behind the tender enabling the Paddington-Bristol run to be non-stop.
(Adrian Knowles)

5043 on arrival at Paddington some 44 minutes early, after running the 118 miles from Bristol via Badminton as the *Bristolian* in 109 minutes 58 seconds without exceeding 80mph, 17 April 2010.
(Adrian Knowles)

5043 stands at Birmingham Moor Street ready to depart on its non-stop run to Paddington, 6 April 2013. (Bob Meanley)

5043 on arrival at Euston No.1 platform with a railtour from Birmingham, 21 May 2010. (Bob Meanley)

5043 Earl of Mount Edgcumbe at speed on the Red Dragon railtour passing Bredon just north of Ashchurch, 11 March 2017. (Robin Coombes)

5043 *Earl* of Mount Edgcumbe at Stafford station, returning to Tyseley after a railtour, on the evening of 18 August 2012. (Robin Coombes)

5043 Earl of Mount Edgcumbe sprints along the sea wall in this classic view of the approach to Dawlish station with the return Cornishman railtour, 28 April, 2012. (Robin Coombes)

Above: 5043 at Ribblehead with a southbound Carlisle-Hellifield railtour, 20 March 2012. (Les Nixon)

Opposite: A view from the fireman's seat as 5043 approaches Paddington station, March 2012. (Bob Meanley)

5043 crossing the Forth Bridge during its Scottish railtour weekend, May 2012. (Bob Meanley Collection)

5043 at Stirling on its *Caledonian* tour from Crewe to Edinburgh-Linlithgow-Stirling-Crewe, 27 May 2012. (David Maidment)

5043 at Stirling – note the buffer marking, 27 May 2012.
(David Maidment)

5043 bearing the *Cheltenham Flyer* headboard of the 1930s at the Tyseley Open Day, 22 June 2013. (David Maidment)

Above left: **A view** from the driver's seat as 5043 approaches Crewe with a Birmingham – Llandudno excursion in May 2014. (Bob Meanley)

Above right: **First Great** Western's Matthew Golton with Bob Meanley at Gloucester on the occasion of 5043's *Cheltenham Flyer* run of 11 May 2011. (Tony Streeter/Bob Meanley Collection)

5043 with the GUV water cart and support coach at Plymouth North Road ready to replicate 7029's 9 May 1964 run from Plymouth to Bristol, 10 May 2014. (David Maidment)

Bob Meanley and his son, Alastair, pose on the footplate of 5043 at Banbury station, c2011. (Bob Meanley Collection)

Chapter 6
5051 *EARL BATHURST*

The information about 5051 in preservation is drawn from a 1980 *Railway World* article by the Great Western Society General Manager, Mick Dean, with additional information from GWS member, Peter Chatman.

5051 was built in May 1936 at a cost of £4,848 plus £952 for a 4,000 gallon tender, named *Dryslwyn Castle*, and allocated to Landore where it spent its entire career until the closure of the shed to construct Landore diesel depot on the site. It was renamed *Earl Bathurst* in August 1937. It was then briefly shedded at Neath and Llanelli before withdrawal in May 1963, having achieved 1,316,659 miles in traffic. It was purchased in 1969 by John Mynors from the Woodham Bros. scrapyard at Barry for £3,000 together with a 4,000 gallon Collett tender 2933 from 6989 and left the yard in February 1970, now in the ownership of the Great Western Society, and arrived at the Didcot Centre, brought by Hymek D7052 with a spare 3,500 gallon tender destined for use with 7808 *Cookham Manor*.

It was stripped down, removing fittings, cleating and lagging but overhaul and restoration had to wait while the GWS volunteers tackled three 2-cylinder GW engines, 6998, 7808 and 5900. Some work was carried out on the tender until 1975 when a decision was made to exchange the tender with 5900's as that locomotive was ready for main line running apart from its tender. The new tender for 5051 was Collett 2804 but needing complete overhaul. 5051 entered the lifting shop in May 1976 and its complete overhaul began. The boiler and cab were removed with a 50 ton electric hoist and 6-ton auxiliary jib crane respectively, an inspection by a BR boiler inspector undertaken and boiler repairs commenced. Boiler HA 6661 was built in 1938 for 5074 and converted to an HB type later and was fitted to 5051 during its last Works visit in June 1961. Seventy small tubes (out of 197) had to be replaced and seventeen riveted stays were also wasted and needed renewing. Boiler work was completed in September 1977.

The motion was removed from the frames and examined, and the wheels were also removed from the frames. The motion and axleboxes were sent to BREL Swindon Works for repair and the driving wheels for journal turning. The connecting and coupling rods were machine polished to remove the pitting that occurred during the engine's long sojourn at Barry in the open. While at Swindon the driving axles were ultrasonically tested, and a certificate was issued. At Didcot, the frames were cleaned from their liberal coating of grease, oil, ash, coal and brake dust which had helped to protect them and painted black outside and red inside. After return of the driving axles and motion from Swindon, the bogie was dismantled, and the wheels, axleboxes and springs sent to Swindon for complete treatment. The ashpan was repaired at Didcot. The boiler was lifted back onto the frames in November 1977 after being hydraulically tested in October and a static steam test carried out in December. Safety valves, injector and pressure gauges were restored and apart from one minor stay leakage, all was well.

In the meantime, repairs on the tender 2804 had to be undertaken, the tank removed and the axles despatched to Swindon for attention. By May 1978, the bogie had been returned, but it was found that the axleboxes were too tight in the horns, and the necessary rectification was carried out at Didcot. The Didcot hoist was under repair so other work not requiring the hoist was undertaken. As a result of regulations tightening after a superheater flue failure on Didcot's 0-6-2T 6697, 5051's remaining small tubes were replaced and five new superheater flues acquired. The other nine superheater flues were ultrasonically tested and passed muster and given clearance until January 1980. Various other work was carried out during this period – rebuilding the engine and tender dragboxes, rebushing the brakegear, and work on the cab and splashers, including replacement of the brass beading which had disappeared at Barry.

In March 1979, the engine's owner, John Mynors, died but his widow and family decided to retain ownership and gave the GWS the necessary financial support to complete the task. The volunteer workforce was challenged to complete the overhaul by the end of 1979 and with the help of the Didcot based '38 Mob' (restoring GW 2-8-0 3822) and the volunteers restoring 2-6-2T 6106, final repairs to the engine and tender were finished despite last minute problems finding copper pipework. The boiler was hydraulically tested in November and work continued by the volunteer gangs, day and night, to meet the deadline. The repaired tender from 5900 (originally bought for 5051) was to be borrowed back and 5051 was lit up for the first time on 1 December. Problems emerged and the regulator valve refused to open. After repair another steaming attempt was made on 2 December, but this time the injectors refused to operate so the fire was thrown out once again. Steam was successfully raised on 8 December, and running-in commenced. A successful steam test certificate was issued on 9 December. Road tests and inspection by a BR inspector to clear for main line running identified further problems (a tender bearing had run hot during the tests and there had been injector problems) and the proposed first railtour with 5051 scheduled for 12 January 1980 was postponed for

5051 *Earl Bathurst* drifts past Cardiff Goods Depot with the 8am Neyland-Paddington express, September 1958. Note that it is still equipped with the original Castle style tall chimney.
(John Hodge)

just a week. Final steam tests took place on 7 January, and the next day was spent running on the GWS demonstration line. It then went to Swindon to go on the weigh table for getting its weight balance right. A new tender axlebox was fitted, but further tests on 13 January still showed problems and the tender box still running warm. However, it quickly showed signs of cooling and a decision was made to run with 5051's tender and not borrow that from 5900. A final running-in trip took place with the 10-coach GWS vintage train on 16 January and after sustained running at 60mph between Oxford and Didcot all was well and the planned first railtour with 5051, *The Phoenix*, from Didcot to Stratford-on-Avon and back duly took place successfully on Saturday, 19 January with 5051 sporting the *Drysllwyn Castle* nameplates preferred by its owner. A further run took place on 26 January, the last with the GWS vintage train, starting from Paddington with a BBC film crew in attendance and 5051 taking over at Didcot.

Further tours took place and 5051 was a regular performer in the GW 150 anniversary celebrations of 1985, for some of which it reverted to its first name, *Drysllwyn Castle*. On 1 September it was paired with 7029 with an 11-coach 440ton gross train and ran from Plymouth to Newton Abbot in 54¾ minutes climbing to Dainton from Totnes at a minimum of 24mph, both locomotives blowing off steam at the summit, arriving there nearly ten minutes early. Both engines took water at Exeter, slowed to 20 (pws) at Tiverton and then passed Whiteball at 53mph with nothing over 70 on the descent. The train was then delayed as the hot axlebox detector near Taunton was triggered in error. Departure from Taunton was thus 6 minutes late and the train was routed via Weston-super-Mare and with a last burst of 75mph through Yatton, it was over 4 minutes early into Bristol.

It has been paired with both Collett and Hawksworth 4,000 gallon tenders. It was initially restored in GW livery, then subsequently in BR early lined green. Its boiler certificate expired in 2008 and it is currently on static display at Didcot awaiting repair to follow the completion of 4079.

5051 (with *Drysllwyn Castle* **chalked on the splasher) in Dai Woodham's scrapyard at Barry being prepared for removal to Didcot, 13 February 1970.** (GW Trust)

Hymek D7052, hauling 5051 and a Churchward 3,500 gallon tender to Didcot, makes an inspection break at Lydney, 13 February 1970. (GW Trust)

5051's boiler being lifted from its frames in the Didcot lifting shop, June 1976. (GW Society)

5051's frames with the boiler in the background before further stripping and cleaning began, June 1976. (GW Society)

5051's frame being lifted to remove the driving wheels, August 1976. Some of the Society's locomotive restoration gang are in attendance. (GW Society)

5051 under repair and restoration in the workshop at the Didcot Railway Centre, 1978. (David Maidment)

5051 as restored at Didcot in 1979 in the original 1936 condition and livery with its original *Dryslwyn Castle* nameplates, January 1980. (Peter Zabek)

5051 at Didcot at the end of 1979. (*GW Echo*)

5051 in the weighbridge shop at Swindon, 10 January 1980. (GW Trust)

5051 climbing Hatton Bank with the final run of the GW vintage train set from Paddington to Stratford-on-Avon, *The Sunset,* 26 January 1980. (W.A. Sharman)

5051, and support coach, taking water at Newport High Street at 2am on return from Shrewsbury, 14 July 1983. (GW Trust)

5051, renamed *Drysllwyn Castle* (leading), and 7029 *Clun Castle* double-head the GW 150 Special railtour from Plymouth to Bristol, climbing Dainton bank, September 1985. (David Maidment)

5051 *Drysllwyn* Castle (renamed from *Earl Bathurst* for the occasion) at Exeter St David's when piloting 7029 on a GW 150 anniversary railtour from Plymouth to Bristol, September 1985.
(David Maidment)

5051 *Earl* Bathurst on display at Toddington at a Gloucestershire Warwickshire Railway Gala event, c2012.
(David Maidment)

5051 *Earl Bathurst* restored and with Hawksworth tender, at the Great Western Centre, Didcot, 27 September 2016. Note the removal of the capuchin on the chimney to meet the current main line height restriction. Also in the photo from left to right are 6998, 5322 and right of 5051, 3822. (David Maidment)

Chapter 7
5080 *DEFIANT*
(BOB MEANLEY)

5080 was built in May 1939 and named *Ogmore Castle*. It was renamed *Defiant* in January 1941 and spent most of its career at Cardiff Canton until 1955 when it moved to Landore and on to Llanelli after that depot's closure. It was withdrawn in April 1963 and moved to the Woodham Bros. scrapyard in October. It was purchased by 7029 Clun Castle Ltd. in 1974 to provide spare parts for the Tyseley Castles 7029 and 7027. Following delivery to Tyseley it stood around the yard in basic scrapyard condition for around 11 years. Some greasing of exposed bearing surfaces did take place but otherwise it continued weathering in the open air.

During the 1985 celebration of the GWR 150th anniversary, talk turned to overhauling another Castle and putting it back in working order. 7027 had over the preceding decade seen various repairs undertaken as time and finance permitted and would normally have been the candidate for any acceleration of work. The proposal coincided with the then Birmingham Railway Museum which had the opportunity of becoming involved with the Birmingham City Council in the promotion of a Job Creation scheme which eventually became one of the largest in the West Midlands. It was therefore proposed that the restoration of a Castle would provide a suitable object of a discrete scheme. This all rather coincided with a growing desire to restore a genuine GWR built Castle and as it was far more complete than 5043, 5080 was chosen for the project. It has to be recalled that at the time, the repair of 5043 was considered to be an impossible dream. Approval was given and a team of new employees was engaged. Few of those involved had any real experience although some talented machinists were engaged in making parts for it. The Museum was fortunate to have the involvement of Don Green who had been foreman of Worcester works in its closing days and Don consequently brought his experience going back to Swindon in the 1930s to bear and oversaw the repairs to the frames and tender. The boiler work was undertaken with somewhat less supervision and that would later cause problems. As a piece of project management, it achieved its objective of returning 5080 to working order in just over a year and a half. In those days, Tyseley possessed far less resource and skill base than it does now and much heavy machining work was done externally, the bogie in particular being overhauled at Swindon. Many of the parts repaired for 7027 were transferred to 5080, and poor old 7027 was turned out to the yard to make way for 5080.

Following completion, some running in was undertaken away from the main line, and eventually it was turned out for its first trial trip on the main line, which sadly did not go well, with one of the Swindon repaired axleboxes running hot a few miles after leaving Tyseley. It eventually ran its first excursion from Tyseley to Didcot in 1988, but it then experienced further issues with a tender axlebox and a broken coupled wheel underkeep oil filler which resulted in failures to work trains. Worse came as it began to suffer persistent leakage from the superheater flue tube expansions and that issue resulted in its removal from main line operations, mainly because various issues at the museum precluded the expense of carrying out the necessary re-tubing. It was found that away from the extreme conditions of main line working, the tubes could be persuaded to behave themselves, and so it entered a new career working on preserved lines for a while. It spent time at the Severn Valley, Mid Hants, Llangollen, and Great Central lines in particular, as well as a period at Quainton Road steam centre.

The final stage of its preservation career to date came when the Museum launched its incredibly successful 'Drive a Loco' courses, on which it became the star turn. Hundreds of people took the opportunity for a turn on the regulator handle. We met a great number of interesting people who came to drive it, and in particular a later conversation with an MP who rose to be the Secretary of State for Transport revealed that he too had done a course at Tyseley on it! Eventually of course it ran to the end of its boiler period in 1997 and was laid up to await an opportunity to take it in for repair. It stood in storage for a while until we were approached by the people at Quainton Road to ask if they could have the loan of it for a while as the centre piece of their spectacular newly erected Rewley Road station building. It was a wonderful opportunity to have it placed somewhere warm and dry with volunteers who would look after it and explain it to visitors. After a number of years at Quainton, the trustees at Tyseley decided that they would like to have it returned during May 2017 and launched a fund to return it to working order. To date that fund has raised a not insignificant sum of money, but it is currently insufficient to repair it and the engine once more languishes in storage, although a start has been made on the overhaul of its tender which now requires a new tender tank and heavy repairs to its frame. The fund remains open and continues to grow.

Canton's 5080 *Defiant* at the head of the 5.55pm Paddington-Swansea *Red Dragon*, 21 April 1953. 5080 has the original taller chimney and Hawksworth tender. (R.O. Tuck/Rail Archive Stephenson)

Canton's 5080 at Shrewsbury waiting to take over a Manchester-Cardiff train, 30 June 1955. (R.O. Tuck/Rail Archive Stephenson)

Landore's 5080 *Defiant* passing Canton shed with the 8.55am Paddington-West Wales express, c1959. (Alan Jarvis/Gerald Nichols Collection)

5080 *Defiant* part restored in GW 1930s livery at Tyseley, 16 July 1987. (Chris Morrison)

Landore's 5080 *Defiant* passing Canton with probably the 11.55am Paddington-Swansea, c1961. (Alan Jarvis/Gerald Nichols Collection)

Chapter 8
7027 THORNBURY CASTLE
(BY BOB MEANLEY)

7027 was built in September 1949 and was based at Old Oak Common from 1951 to 1960, when it was transferred to Worcester, from where it was withdrawn in August 1963. It was initially purchased for scrap by Woodham Bros. but sold to 7029 Clun Castle Ltd. in 1972. At that time, it was probably in the best condition of the five Castles at Barry. During the mid-1970s some restoration work began on it. One of the issues with the Castles in Barry was that there was an insufficiency of connecting rods for all of the locomotives and 7027 was one of the victims left without rods. As part of the restoration efforts a set of new rods were made by Indian Railways at their Chitteranjan workshops and were duly fitted to the engine. At the time of writing, they are

7027 *Thornbury Castle* of Laira, in filthy condition even though less than two years old, at Neath on a Swansea-Plymouth train, 4 August 1951. It was transferred to Old Oak Common just a couple of months later and remained there until 1960 when it moved to Worcester for the last WR steam-hauled express passenger services. (F.K. Davies Collection/John Hodge Collection)

7027 Thornbury Castle at Swindon Works after a heavy overhaul, 11 September 1955. (F.M. Gates/F.K. Davies & John Hodge Collections)

7027 Thornbury Castle passes the GW Society centre on the Didcot avoiding curve with the Up *Cathedrals Express*, 29 March 1962. (Charles Gordon-Stuart/GW Trust)

A splendid oil painting by Philip Hawkins of 7027 *Thornbury Castle* departing from Paddington with a Worcester train. This view, from platform 1 at Paddington, was mainly only known to railwaymen and those members of the public with rather more than a passing interest in railways. Today this view is virtually the same, but time has seen a drastic change in motive power with Hitachi Class 800/2 bi-mode units taking the place of such magnificent locomotives. (Courtesy of Philip D. Hawkins GRA)

currently fitted to 5080 as there are still not enough in existence. During 1985, a decision was made to restore 5080, mainly because it was a genuine GWR engine rather than a later BR built version. Many of the fittings and boiler mountings acquired for 7027 were transferred to 5080, and sadly the condition of 7027 was allowed to deteriorate once more. Several attempts were made to re-start the restoration before Pete Waterman made an offer for it which was reluctantly accepted. Again, early advances proved to be a false dawn and the engine spent a number of years once more gently rusting in a siding at the Crewe Heritage Centre. It moved to the Peak Railway in 2016. In July of that year, it was purchased by Jon Jones-Pratt who intended to restore the engine to main line standards and it moved in 2018 to the West Somerset Railway at Williton for restoration. However, it was in a queue and unlikely to receive early attention, so in 2020 it was again sold to a private individual who intends to restore it for use on the Great Central Railway at Loughborough. At the time of writing, a promising start has once more taken place and the engine seems to at last have some promise of return to working order.

7027 in unrestored state at Tyseley, 1975.
(Bryan Holden)

The unrestored body of 7027 *Thornbury Castle* stored at the Crewe Heritage Centre while owned by Pete Waterman, 1997.
(Author's Collection)

The hulk of 7027 at the Peak Railway, c2016.
(Author's Collection)

Chapter 9
7029 CLUN CASTLE
(BOB MEANLEY)

The Great Western's fleet of Castles steadily grew, with many years during the decade prior to the Second World War seeing a batch of ten Castles entering service, until there were 131 examples. The advent of war brought a temporary halt to further construction. Following the cessation of hostilities in 1945 the company embarked on a programme for the construction of forty further Castles to replace the time expired examples of their predecessor 'Star' class, culminating in the final batch of ten locomotives built under the auspices of the newly formed British Railways during 1950. By this time the class had been in service for twenty-seven years and yet was still considered perfectly good enough to merit further construction. History has shown that this decision was perfectly sound and that with the modifications which resulted from the ground breaking work of Swindon's renowned development and testing section, they would continue to prove that size for size, they remained the equal of any similar locomotive which British Railways would possess until steam traction was phased out in the mid-1960s.

Included in the 1950 lot (as Swindon called such batches) was a locomotive numbered 7029 and named *Clun Castle* continuing the now traditional style of naming this class after various historic castles around the GWR system, in this instance a small castle constructed in the Welsh borders by the Norman, Picot de Say, started during the late eleventh century. The castle was developed by the Fitzalan family before being laid waste by Owain Glyn Dwr's campaigns during the early 1400s. Locomotive 7029 was however destined for a somewhat shorter initial career in service, being first allocated to Newton Abbot depot where it hauled various services including the *Torbay Express* from Paddington to Torquay, Paignton and Kingswear. It turned out to be a not particularly distinguished member of the class during the first ten years of its life but settled down to steady work which did little to draw the attention of enthusiasts of the day, in effect it was just another Castle. All that was about to begin to change with the fitting of a higher superheat boiler and double chimney during 1959. It was now about to join the 'Super Castle' league and following its last major overhaul (Heavy General repair in railway parlance) it was re-allocated to London's famous Old Oak Common depot in July 1962. This depot tended to have a reputation of housing only the best of the Castles.

In the lottery of the final days of steam, 7029 somehow survived to be the last Great Western designed express passenger locomotive in service on British Railways, when on 31 December 1965 it worked its last service train from Gloucester to Cheltenham, 128 years and 3 days after the Great Western steamed its first engine, the Tayleur built broad gauge 2-2-2 *Vulcan*. During 7029's last two years in service it became something of a celebrity after it was selected to take part in the famed high speed special run of 9 May 1964, which BR operated to celebrate the passing from service of the Castles. During that run it had broken the Plymouth to Bristol speed record for steam; and it went on to work the last scheduled steam hauled service out of Paddington as well as the last steam hauled special to leave that station.

During early 1964, the Western Region's senior management began to consider arranging one final celebration of the class with a special train to be worked from Paddington to Plymouth, returning to London via Bristol. Some quite exciting trials were held to determine which of the Castles were considered to be in a good enough condition to work this train, which was expected to see the sort of high speed running for which the class had become famous. These trials were conducted over the route from Paddington to Worcester which was the last route to see regular operation of the Castles on express passenger services and rumour had it that the magic 'ton' was achieved with several of these engines in the area between Chipping Campden and Honeybourne. After several weeks, the Western Region's mechanical and running inspectors had concluded a ranking of the locomotives which had been trialled, with the best three being selected to haul various sections of the special train and several more being delegated as standbys at points along the route in case of trouble. It was a sign of the times and the state of the average locomotive that such things were considered, and it proved to be a wise decision.

On 9 May 1964, the train set out from Paddington for Plymouth headed by 4079 *Pendennis Castle* of 1925 trials fame. Approaching Lavington at almost 100 miles per hour, a large section of the firegrate collapsed, shedding a considerable amount of the fire into the ashpan and out under the train onto the track. Brought to a stand by an emergency brake application, the train then limped in to Westbury where the loco was removed from the train and replaced by 'Hall' Class loco 6999 *Capel Dewi Hall*. Whilst the 'Hall' put up an astonishing performance taking the train forward to Taunton, the passengers had come for Castle haulage and so the Hall was replaced at Taunton by 7025 *Sudeley Castle*, which had been one of the engines rostered for standby duty, and which took the train on to Plymouth. After a break for passengers in Plymouth, the return journey started out from Plymouth Millbay station headed by 7029 *Clun Castle*, which was about to emerge from the shadow of being just another Castle to become one of the most famous examples of the class.

Manned by men from Plymouth's Laira depot, the crew consisted of driver Harold Roach, firemen Bill Rundle and Bill Watts, with Headquarters inspector Bill Andress overseeing the operation. Communication must have been interesting with three 'Bills' on the footplate! Two firemen were considered necessary as the men had become more accustomed to the somewhat less taxing operation of diesel locomotives in recent times and the medical officer apparently considered that it would be necessary to provide two firemen to share the heavy work required in firing such a high-speed run. The details of the run have been published many times and it will suffice to say that after the passage of the South Devon banks, the passengers were to become aware that something special was happening as the train stormed over the summit of Whiteball bank. Hopes were high that the magical ton might be achieved on the downhill run through Wellington where 3440 *City of Truro* had allegedly achieved such a figure exactly sixty years before, but a special dispensation from the Civil Engineer relaxing the 80mph speed limit at Wellington was unfortunately not relayed to the locomotive inspector, so 80mph it was, much to the disgust of driver Roach so we are told! Beyond Wellington, the train accelerated to 97mph before Taunton and again ran at speeds in the 90s across the Somerset levels before arriving at Bristol in an overall time of 133 minutes and 10 seconds, in the process setting a record for steam traction between Plymouth and Bristol which was to stand for the next fifty years. The locomotive had done so well on the journey, (largely due to its fastidious preparation at Laira by Mechanical Inspector Harold Cook during the preceding week) that the crews suggested that it should continue with the train to Paddington. Sadly, we can only conjecture what might have been if it had been allowed to continue, for the 'powers that be' deemed that the booked locomotive 5054 *Earl of Ducie* must take up the train.

However, 9 May 1964 would prove to be the most important day in 7029's existence as it would ultimately ensure that it would pass into preservation rather than a South Wales scrapyard. For the moment, it was still just another engine in BR's inventory, and the following day would see the newly anointed record breaker heading a banana train from Avonmouth to Acton in London; how the mighty were fallen in those days. During the course of the momentous journey from Plymouth, the idea of saving *Clun* for preservation had occurred to two of the passengers, John Southern and Jack Trounson, and they pondered the idea of a fund to raise the purchase price demanded by BR. In the event that would turn out to be £3,000, a pretty large sum in those days. We shall return to this suggestion shortly.

In the meantime, 7029 began to be something of a celebrity, and by the spring of 1965 it was one of only four surviving members of the class, and it was in by far the best condition of the four. Requests for its use on railtours grew and so did its use on special occasions. During 1965 it became the engine of choice for a variety of enthusiast trains, which ran to far flung destinations including a ground breaking special run to Nottingham. Perhaps the most important event was when it was used to haul the last ever steam hauled service train to depart from Paddington station, and again when it was used to power the Western Region's final (and last) special steam train to leave Paddington to celebrate the passing of steam traction. By this time, 7029 was not only the sole survivor of the 171 Castles but had also become the last GWR designed passenger engine to be in service on British Railways, and it would soldier on for another month or so, its final working apparently a Gloucester to Cheltenham train on New Year's Eve 1965. The following day would see 7029 withdrawn from service and the effective elimination of all steam traction on the Western Region, but 7029 was about to start a whole new life, where it would be truly embedded in the 'Castle' Hall of Fame.

Towards the end of 1965, talk turned once more to the preservation of the engine. Such matters had first surfaced on board the 1964 high speed special following its spirited run from Plymouth to Bristol. It built on the earlier discussion between Jack Trounson and John Southern, the two West Country enthusiasts who were passengers on the 9 May train. Trounson in particular had serious steam connections, evidently counting the renowned Richard Trevithick amongst his ancestors. They consequently founded a fund to purchase the locomotive which did indeed raise some money, but sadly nowhere near enough to raise the £3,000 which British Railways demanded as a sale price. However, salvation was at hand. I recall the late Pat Whitehouse telling me that at a meeting with the then BR-WR General Manager he was told that the regional management would like to see it saved but were unable to do so themselves. The GM (Gerry Fiennes) suggested that they thought that Pat was just the man to do it, doubtless due to the number of smaller engine purchases with which he had been involved in the previous year or so (4555, 1420, 1638, etc). Pat duly got together with Jack Trounson and John Southern and with the involvement of other sponsors including the well-known Black Country iron founder, the late Tom Hunt, the necessary purchase price was raised.

The team very quickly found themselves the owners of a slightly careworn, but nevertheless operational GWR Castle. Now, it is all very well buying a large express passenger engine, but what do you then do with it to comply with the BR contract of sale condition to remove it from their property? Thought turned to the idea of following the small engines to Devon and parking it on the nascent Dart Valley Railway, albeit with the realisation that it was far too heavy to work on the little railway. Nothing daunted, it was decided that the best option might be to stable it for the time being on BR property. Pat had form for this as 4555 had been stabled at Tyseley for almost two years during 1964/65 and during that time some rock solid relationships had been established with senior local management. 1965 had been a bright spot in a somewhat depressing period at Tyseley due to the presence of the preserved engines destined for the Dart Valley line, but by the end of that year they had all departed for Devon. It was not long before 7029 found itself stabled in the Tyseley roundhouse. Initial thoughts were that 7029 would nevertheless become a static exhibit at the embryonic Dart Valley Railway, but a basically operational Castle was a little too much for itchy fingers, and 'what if we…..' soon transcended into the engine finding itself steaming around Tyseley shed yard, progressing to various somewhat anonymous goods workings on the Birmingham to Banbury line.

At the beginning of 1966 steam traction was just a year away from its demise in the Birmingham area. The former Great Western depot at Tyseley was a rundown shell of its former self, the goods engine side of the roundhouse and the lifting shop (or factory as it was known to the men) had been demolished and just a memory. The void left by the demolition of the goods side was enclosed by a scaffolding and corrugated iron wall to keep out the worst of the weather, and the shed took on the air of a bomb site. All of the GWR tender engines and big tanks had also disappeared and all that lingered on were a small handful of pannier tanks still occupied on shunting and local freights, and which were destined to become the last GWR engines in service on BR in late 1966. They had however been replaced by a somewhat more noble successor, the last working Castle, 7029 *Clun Castle*, and it would have a home in the dilapidated roundhouse for another two years or so. Being in a live steam shed it is no surprise that *Clun* was soon steamed once more and repairs were carried out to remedy various defects, after all there was a residual stock of various spare parts which were hardly likely to find further use. A group of volunteers was formed and expeditions went to other sheds such as Leamington, Banbury and Worcester to acquire further supplies.

In recent times, 4555 in particular had enjoyed numerous forays onto the main line working service trains, even to the extent of working evening trains from Snow Hill to Knowle and Dorridge. It was perhaps inevitable that 7029 would once more escape from captivity and that duly happened in late spring 1966 when it started appearing on goods trains between Birmingham and Banbury. Strangely, these had a habit of coinciding with days when Pat was returning from business in London, so he was able to enjoy the odd ride back from Banbury on the engine. The engine looked equally as sad as the shed – somewhat grubby and without name and number plates.

Over the winter of 1966/67, the engine was repainted and restored to pristine condition by painters from the Whitehouse family's construction company. The livery adopted was the source of some interest as it was painted in the BR version of lined green correct for its construction in 1950 but carrying Great Western lettering and the company's twin shields badge in place of the BR badge on the tender. The reasoning behind this was that BR were not happy with privately owned engines carrying BR insignia, hence the adoption of the GWR company branding to overcome BR's objection. One little known facet of this repaint was that the engine's frames were painted in a dark red resembling that which had been recently applied to 4079. It lasted for only a few days at the most and was quickly repainted in the correct black. The emphasis on carrying out this renovation was an engagement to work special trains to commemorate the cessation of through services between Paddington and Birkenhead in March 1967.

1967 saw the start of 7029's second career when it once more started to work special trains, in particular the last ever trains to work through to Birkenhead Woodside, culminating in it being the last GWR engine to work a passenger train into Birmingham's famous and much-loved Snow Hill station. The Birkenhead trains brought to a close main line services through Birmingham Snow Hill station. On 4 March, 7029 worked a special from Banbury to Chester whilst 4079 worked another train from Didcot to Chester. The following day, 7029 was out again working a special from Tyseley to Birkenhead. Bookings were so heavy that an extra train was run in the charge of LMS Black 5 No. 44680. During the layover at Birkenhead, the two engines were changed over so that 7029 worked the second train's return to Birmingham, where it became the last steam hauled train to arrive at Snow Hill before the station was closed to through traffic later that evening. During the course of that return journey, problems arose. The first was that the fireman was experiencing difficulty in firing the loco, a situation which was saved by Tyseley fireman Bernard Rainbow stepping up to save the day as he was fortunately a passenger on the train. The second was a potentially serious mechanical issue with a stripped thread on one of the inside cylinder valve spindles, which fortunately just held out long enough to make the return to Birmingham. That problem was resolved by BR Tyseley shed sending fitters in a van to Woodhams where a deal was done to purchase the two inside valve spindles from 7027, thereby starting something of a tradition of acquiring spares, and ultimately further engines for spares, from Barry.

Once repaired and back in good order, 7029 soon embarked on the round of railtours in the east and north of the country taking in the

East Coast main line to Newcastle, the West Coast main line to Carlisle and the Settle and Carlisle (see earlier, pages 16 to 19). Sadly, this enterprise was brought to an end by the absolute ban on private steam locomotives imposed by BR in November 1967, so it was a case that 7029 became imprisoned at Tyseley for the time being. It had been joined at Tyseley by a new addition to the collection, the LMS Jubilee 5593 *Kolhapur,* and over the next few years the two engines, together with a further addition in the shape of LMS 'Black 5' 5428, made isolated forays either singly or collectively to various open days at Bristol Bath Road, Allerton, Cricklewood, and Stratford depots. They also featured in the spectacularly successful open day at Tyseley depot in September 1968, when around 18,000 visitors attended, due to the wave of steam euphoria following cessation of steam traction on BR. Further Tyseley open days were held in subsequent years, but the 1968 attendance was never repeated probably due to the upsurge in private line activity providing steam action for the masses. That was to change at the autumn open day in 1971 when it was attended by GWR King class 6000 *King George V* as part of its steam ban-busting tour with the Bulmer's cider train. This laid the path for the 'Return to Steam' initiative, and 7029 was selected to work the first public charter train of this new post-steam era. *Clun* had a job once more! During this period, the engine had been one of the primary factors in the far-seeing decision to develop a maintenance facility around it at Tyseley and over the years this has now become the very substantial Tyseley Locomotive Works, which effectively has the capacity and ability to build new locomotive frames and boilers, very much a whole locomotive in fact.

Steam locomotives can be very demanding things to maintain. In particular, regulations require boilers to be thoroughly overhauled at maximum intervals of ten years and 7029 has seen various periods in storage and under such repairs in the intervening years. In between repairs it had seen much use on the main line and on preserved lines, perhaps the best-known workings were operating the first ever train in BR's 'Return to Steam' programme in 1972, and its outings during 1985, when in celebration of the 150th anniversary of the GWR it roamed far and wide across lines of the old company, even penetrating into Cornwall as far as St Blazey (Par).

David Maidment reports that his friend Alastair Wood timed 7029 on a heavy twelve coach 460ton gross loaded train on 24 May 1986 on the Hereford-Newport section of the *Welsh Marches Express,* taking over from 3440 *City of Truro* and 6000 *King George V* that had worked from Shrewsbury. After a slow start as the engine warmed up, 7029 was opened out after Pontrilas and surmounted the steep climb to Llanvihangel at 36mph and rushed down through Abergavenny at 73mph arriving at Pontypool Road, despite a p-way slack near Nantyderry, ten minutes early. After taking the curve at Maindee East Junction, 7029 continued to Gloucester at a steady 65mph along the level stretch beside the Severn and finally, Alastair noted, with a 'flail' up the 1 in 335 to MP 118, 7029 actually accelerating to 69mph. Arrival in Gloucester was five minutes early. The following year, Paul Walker recorded a log (taken from the Rail Performance Society's archives) on the Sunday excursion from Marylebone to Stratford-on-Avon and back. The date was 29 May 1988. There was engineering work involving 'single line working' before High Wycombe but 7029 roared out of there with its 395/425 ton train accelerating to 59mph in 2½ miles and sustaining 47/52mph on the climb to Saunderton summit, and stopped at Princes Risborough having gained three minutes over the 8.2 mile run. On the return journey, problems were encountered at Banbury with a station overrun and then dragging brakes on departure making the train 25 minutes late passing Bicester but with 72mph after and 57 at Saunderton summit and ignoring the planned water stop at Princes Risborough as unnecessary, High Wycombe was reached three and Marylebone seven minutes early.

But fortunes wane for engines and organisations and this was true for both 7029 and what had become the Birmingham Railway Museum. Around the time of the expiry of 7029's last boiler certificate, the BRM had been enduring some hard times and had just begun the long process of re-establishing itself on what were now the main lines of Railtrack. Many years of use on both main and preserved lines had caused considerable deterioration in the overall condition of the engine despite several periodic repairs, and it was certainly no longer in the condition that it was when purchased from BR. It became apparent that nothing short of the sort of general repair which Swindon Works used to regularly carry out would suffice to bring the loco back to the condition required for main line operation in the twenty-first century, and the time was not right to start such a repair; indeed, the funds were not available to do so. Tyseley Locomotive Works had successfully returned 4965 *Rood Ashton Hall* to main line service three years earlier and it was proving to be something of a gem. The consequence of the success of that repair had brought about an intent to return the derelict hulk of 5043 *Earl of Mount Edgcumbe* to working order. To some extent this usurped 7029, and this was particularly so when 5043 was to participate during 2014 in a 50th anniversary re-run of 7029's famous 1964 record run. In the hands of Driver Ray Churchill and fireman Alastair Meanley, 5043 was to shave over three minutes from 7029's record Plymouth to Bristol time despite having a heavier train, perhaps leaving the challenge of unfinished business? Nevertheless, the success of 5043's re-introduction to service brought about not only the will to properly repair 7029, but also a revenue stream to help fund such a repair. 7029 was also to reap the benefits of the expanded capabilities and new facilities at what has become Tyseley Locomotive Works; the new workshop in particular, matched by the growth in skills of its workforce, have meant that the repair process has been able to be accomplished far more effectively than would have been the case even twenty years ago. Nevertheless 7029's repair has still seen an input of over 30,000 man-hours to return it to the condition which will be seen today.

The Repair

We commenced repairs to 7029 during 2010, which was coincidentally the year of celebration for the 175th anniversary of the formation of the Great Western Railway. At the time, 5043 was away carrying the Great Western flag on such memorable events as the first nonstop *Bristolian* expresses to run since 1959. Whilst 5043 and 7029 were effectively much the same in their design, their condition at the onset of repairs were very different. On the one hand, 5043 had been little more than the bare bones of an engine, stripped of most removable components, particularly those made from brass and copper, and bereft of any form of tender. The interesting point was that we did, however, know that there were no preservation era 'fixes' to be overcome; not much remained but what did was pure railway. On the other hand, 7029 was a complete engine with all of its parts intact, as we have always made a point in recent times of not stealing parts from one engine to put on another under restoration. The problem was that it had been a long time since it had seen the inside of Swindon works (almost as long as 5043 in fact) and whilst it had received what were deemed overhauls in the early preservation era, those were in effect little more than intermediate retubing of the boiler, coupled with some mechanical adjustments. Just as with 5080, *Clun* had suffered a certain amount of wear and tear operating on the BRM's 'drive a loco' activities during the late 1990s which provided an essential lifeline to the somewhat rickety finances during that period. By the time that 7029's boiler certificate expired, the 5043 repair was well under way and so 7029 spent almost ten years on the side-lines watching 5043 subsume its erstwhile position as the collection's flagship. It remains to be seen whether 7029 will have the opportunity in the current climate to equal many of 5043's achievements. So what we started with was a somewhat careworn Castle which looked tidy, particularly when shipped to York for static display at the NRM's major event in 2004. In steam days, it was entirely possible to predict the necessity of many repairs to a steam locomotive before the stripping process began, but then, as now, there are always hidden extras which only become apparent when the locomotive is stripped to its component parts. This process always presents surprises - some good, most bad! As it progressed, 7029's repair was no exception to this rule, and it was undoubtedly and entirely at the level that would have been expected of a heavy general classified repair carried out at Swindon Works in the days when steam traction was still a commodity which was highly valued and accorded the very best of attention. We were determined that such a repair would be carried out on the engine for the first time in its preservation career.

Once stripped down to a point where there was virtually nothing left to unbolt, the repair attended to everything which was either known beforehand or which became evident as the repair progressed. The boiler was removed from the frame, the coupled wheels were removed as was the bogie, and all of the valve motion, pistons and valves were taken out. The tender was known to have a somewhat weary tank and front dragbox and that was also stripped to its component parts, with the tank removed, revealing a not unexpected and considerable amount of work.

Once removed from the frame, the boiler was detubed and given a thorough examination to determine the full extent of repairs required. In short, it required the removal and renewal of the smokebox in its entirety, a new front tube plate, repairs to wasted sections of the barrel external to the tube plate, renewal of all crown stays and many steel and copper side stays, renewal of lower sections of the throat plate, large sections on both sides of the wrapper plate, and the shoulders and lower section of the back plate, with repairs also required to the foundation ring. As a result of all this work, the foundation ring was completely re-riveted, in addition to the re-riveting of the firehole. All small boiler tubes together with the superheater flue tubes and elements were renewed. The main steam pipes had been renewed by the Great Central Railway during a loan period there in the 1990s, but radiographic examination of them determined that some of the welds were really not suitable for further use and consequently they were renewed with even more difficulty than was the case when the similar exercise was carried out during 5043's repair. On reassembly of the engine, the smokebox was fitted with our own design of self-cleaning smokebox and spark arrestor screens with which 5043 has been successfully operating for almost nine years. Substantial repairs were also required to the feed water dispersal trays inside the boiler. The normal renewal of all boiler mounting studs, washout plugs, mud doors and fusible plugs was undertaken.

Once the frame had been comprehensively stripped, it gave an opportunity to scrape off all of the old paint to get down to bare metal and also to remove any rust and corrosion in areas not reached by oil thrown up by the wheels and motion. As an aside, the heavy concentrations of oil and dirt form an amazing rust preventative which has carried on doing its job on a number of unrestored ex-Barry engines until quite recent times. Interestingly, the removal of paint revealed that the inside of the frame plates had probably only been repainted once since it was built, and that it was all the rather brownish Venetian red specified by Swindon rather than the mythical bright red incorrectly favoured by many preservationists. It is a matter of fact that we have never yet found any evidence of bright red paint on any ex-Barry frame which we have worked on. Careful inspection of the frame revealed that they required the renewal of much of the rear dragbox, cab floor structure and lower cab sides in order to replace extensively corroded material. The frame stretchers and horns were found to be generally tight, although a small number of cylinder bolts required re-tightening which is not unusual for Castles. As with 5043, the bolts securing the bogie side bearers were renewed as a matter of course.

We were very pleasantly surprised by the general condition of the axleboxes and hornblocks. After applying our gauging gear to the frames we determined that only the rear (or trailing) axlebox guides were sufficiently worn to require correction using our own design of horn grinding machine, all others showing little sign of wear despite the many years since they last received attention at Swindon and the mileage which it has run during the remainder of its BR career added to its preservation era mileage. It was really a comprehensive validation of the value of the Swindon methods for alignment and horn grinding when fully applied and was something of a contradiction of the situation which we found with 5043. Doubtless things were starting to slip with the onset of complete dieselisation and 7029 was fortunate to have been quite evidently repaired to established standards, and that is so obviously why it was one of the engines selected for the 9 May 1964 run. The axleboxes concerned had their liners reset and machined to suit the repaired guides (horns). Due to the usual wear in trailing axleboxes, new bearing brasses were made and fitted to the trailing coupled axleboxes. All of the axle to axle centre distances were checked and reset to the correct dimensions again using gauges manufactured here at Tyseley.

The wheels saw some extensive work, requiring re-tyring at a cost approaching £50,000. It is a mind-focusing thought that each coupled wheel tyre alone cost £3,000 before any work whatsoever was carried out to machine it to size and fit it to the wheelset. Alongside this, the axle bearing journals were examined and rectified as required to bring them back to correct standard and all axleboxes brasses were re-metalled in order to bring them back to new condition as were the axlebox boss face surfaces which were reset to the correct, and very close clearances specified by Swindon.

The cylinders were completely opened up and examined. It is interesting to note that the engine appears to have been fitted with a completely new front end frames and cylinders some time in the late 1950s which may well have a connection with its rejuvenation including the fitting of a double chimney and its promotion to allocation at Old Oak Common. It is interesting to note that this was accompanied by the fitting of a new expansion link cradle carrying the date 1958. At the front end, the cylinders were examined and found to not require re-boring, but the pistons were found to be worn beyond limits so were renewed and re-fitted to re-machined piston rods. All four of the valve chests were also worn beyond limits and were re-bored. The existing valve heads were fit for further use so only the valve rings, valve spindle sleeves and all gland rings and bushes required renewal to bring all back to standard. All four sets of slide bars have been reset and fitted with new packings. This revealed one of the surprises in that at some time in the distant past the top and bottom right hand outside slidebars had been reversed to try to rectify a prior defect in their alignment, and this took not a little effort to rectify and reset them correctly. This misalignment had led to quite extensive wear to a cylinder liner which has had to be renewed as a consequence, and it is obvious that the engine had run for a number of years in BR service with this defect. We returned the slidebars to the correct positions nominated by their stamped identification, and that required the bolt holes in the supporting G iron to be welded up solid and re-drilled to suit the correct position of the slidebars. New bolts were made for all of the slidebars from the correct grade of high tensile steel. This has been our practice for a number of years and its validity was borne out in recent times when a GW engine working on a private railway suffered the breakage of a top slide bar bolt which then dropped down and jammed against the moving crosshead, resulting in extensive damage. Examination of the cylinder drain cocks confirmed them to be beyond repair and they were all renewed.

Looking over the cylinder lubrication system, the cylinder lubricator was completely stripped down, all of the pumps were overhauled, fitted with new seals and pressure tested, and the associated pipework has either been repaired or completely replaced to finally expunge the battered evidence of years of wear and abuse collected during 7029's BR career. One extra which has been fitted to the cylinders is a connection to a steam chest pressure gauge in the cab. Whilst many will say this is not original, in actual fact the Western Region trial fitted two Castles and two Kings with this arrangement, and our installation has been made in exact accordance with the drawings which were made in 1952 for the WR trial of this fitting. According to a contemporary Swindon D.O. report from May 1953, it was not well received by drivers and no further engines were fitted. For the record, the engines originally so fitted were 6006, 6017, 5004, and 5061.

Examination of the valve motion suggested that many of the bronze and white metal bushes required renewal or repair, in particular, all of the connecting and coupling rod bushes were renewed. The coupled wheel crank pins and inside crank pins were all found to be within tolerance and were consequently only re-polished. The pivot pins and bushes for the outside rocker arms which transmit motion to the outside valves needed a substantial amount of work to restore them to good order, again simply because of fair wear and tear. Several of the joint pins within the valve motion have also required replacement, and here this is another example of having to find satisfactory substitute materials as the original grade of nickel bearing case hardening steel is no longer available. The reverser in the cab has required extensive work including renewal of the complex screw therein. Wear and tear causes slackness to develop between the screw and reverser frame and also with the nut connecting the screw to the reversing rod, and this inevitably leads to increasing wear and drastically increased noise levels within the cab due to severe knocking. This can also be exacerbated by increased wear arising in the main reversing shaft bearings. We can only hope that future crews appreciate the considerable time and effort which went into this item.

The boiler mountings and pipework were carefully examined, and in some instances renewed, particularly the driver's brake valve and injector steam pipes in the cab have been replaced. We are very proud of the fact that most of the boiler cleating plates are still the original BR items which were on the loco at the time of its purchase. Much care has gone into repairing these items in order to bring them back to a presentable condition, but in particular one of the boiler barrel panels carried distinct evidence in the form of heavy creasing due to having been folded back to attend to what was probably a repair to an oil or steam pipe buried beneath the cleating in the boiler insulation. This had been clearly visible in some photos of the loco taken during the BR days and indeed, beyond into preservation. We consider that it was worth preserving the original material; after all, there are not too many engines still operating today with original BR cleating panels which look as good as the ones on 7029! One of the main reasons for this is that the quality of the black steel sheet used by the railway is undoubtedly more resistant to corrosion than modern bright cold rolled steel sheet. Despite extensive efforts to prime and rust proof the new panels on 5043, they are already showing signs of corrosion after ten years. In their defence, it is necessary to say that the amount of masonry which falls on them from Network Rail's infrastructure hardly helps the cause.

The tender required considerable work too. The removal of the tank from the frame revealed it to be in a very sorry state which almost suggested its complete renewal. In the end, the TLW team salvaged the side and rear panels after a lot of hard work. For the rest, the whole of the floor, tank top and baffles have been replaced, leaving just the original sides and rear. We fitted sacrificial zinc anodes (as fitted to canal boats) at various points inside the tank as a measure which will hopefully reduce future corrosion rates. Whilst normally out of sight, there is actually a large amount of timber packing of various thicknesses installed between the top of the tender frames and the tank, and this too has been replaced with good quality timber which hopefully will be far more resistant to decay than the original wood used by the GWR (in defence of the GWR the wood was probably not envisaged to last this long?). The frame also required considerable attention to replace corroded metal within the front and rear drag boxes, together with the top plates between tank packing and frame. Wheel tyres and journals were re-machined and associated bearings re-metalled. As with the loco, all bearing springs were repaired or in some instances renewed at a total cost for the whole locomotive and tender of over £12,000.

Finally, the detail work towards the completion of the repair work of necessity focused on repainting and lining the loco in paint which was carefully matched to a 1956 Swindon paint sample panel. Work also focused on fitting the modern electronic systems required before the engine was permitted to operate over Network Rail lines. That included the TPWS system for train protection and warning, data recording equipment and GSMR radio communication equipment, all of which can now add anything up to £100,000 to the repair bill.

The repairs were concluded in late 2017, but sadly the locomotive was unable to return to traffic before the hiatus in Tyseley operations caused by the Vintage Trains board's decision to cease operation with West Coast Railways and to form its own licensed Train Operating Company. In consequence, it saw no use until 2018 and limited operations in 2019 before the Covid pandemic caused further cessation of operations through 2020 and into 2021. It finally resumed operation in late August 2021, but it is only really now beginning to give indications in comparison with 5043. They are said to be similar but the later pattern of hopper ashpan fitted to 7029 definitely causes the fire to burn in a different manner to 5043. It does however remain to be seen if it will enjoy any chance to undertake similar spectacular opportunities to those which 5043 enjoyed during its first ten year period.

Everyone at Tyseley Locomotive Works expected that 7029 would prove equally as good as its shed companion 5043, and that the pair of them would continue to uphold, and indeed further enhance, the reputation of the GWR and its Castle class engines. Of course, none of this would have proved possible without the help and assistance of a great many people – those who donated money to the *Clun* appeal fund, the staff and volunteers of Tyseley Locomotive Works, the West Coast Railways VAB, Network Rail, the TLW suppliers and sub-contractors, together with a host of well-wishers too numerous to mention. Finally, it was an immense source of satisfaction that the TLW works manager, Alastair Meanley, managed this project from beginning to end, producing a result which will hopefully endure for many years.

7029 minus name and numberplates, removed for safe keeping, after withdrawal and purchase by 7029 Clun Castle Ltd, at Tyseley, 15 June 1966.
(MLS Collection)

7029 *Clun* *Castle* after withdrawal at Banbury shed, 29 May 1966.
(Charles Gordon-Stuart/ GW Trust)

7029 Clun Castle • 151

7029 Clun Castle at Swindon Open Day, September 1975.
(Bryan Holden)

Below left: **The frame** of 7029 *Clun Castle* under major overhaul at Tyseley Works, 2016.
(David Maidment)

Below right: **The inside** motion of 7029 awaiting overhaul at Tyseley Works, 2016.
(David Maidment)

Above left: The completed tender frame ready for 7029 in the Tyseley Workshop, October 2013. (Bob Meanley Collection)

Above right: The newly formed firebox shoulder for 7029 at Tyseley Works, December 2013. (Bob Meanley Collection)

Alastair Meanley and his gang of volunteers lift the boiler back into the frames of 7029, 11 June 2016. (Bob Meanley Collection)

Left: **7029's** overhauled trailing axle. Total weight of axlebox and spring assembly is around 7cwt. (Bob Meanley Collection)

Below: **7029** Clun Castle at its first steaming after major overhaul at Tyseley Works, 25 October 2017. (Robin Coombes)

7029, after the hiatus in 2018, pauses on its first test run at Whitlocks End, 19 February 2019. (Bob Sweet)

7029 on its first loaded test run at Songar Grange Farm level crossing, Edstone en route to Small Heath, 21 February 2019. (Bob Sweet)

7029 Clun Castle • 155

7029's inaugural railtour after repair on a Worcester-Birmingham Snow Hill special 1Z20 passing Droitwich, 28 February 2019. (Bob Sweet)

7029 puts on a display of smoke and steam as it passes Droitwich with railtour 1Z71, 07.45 Dorridge-Oxford, 18 May 2019. (Bob Sweet)

7029 passes Cutnall Green with a charter train special with the water-carrying GUV and dead class 47 diesel at the rear, 24 August 2019. (Bob Sweet)

7029 at Norton Junction with the 1Z54 charter train, 24 August 2019. (Bob Sweet)

7029 sails through Dorridge with the Stratford-on-Avon Birmingham *Shakespeare Express*, 15 September 2019. (Bob Sweet)

7029 restarts the 2021 *Shakespeare Express* programme after the pandemic, seen passing Wilmcote, 29 August 2021. (Bob Sweet)

7029 passing Droitwich with a Stephenson Locomotive Society charter train, 08.21 Tyseley-Swindon, with the GUV water-carrier behind the engine, 25 September 2021. (Bob Sweet)

Tyseley's three Castles at an Open Day at the Works, 5080 *Defiant* and 5043 *Earl of Mount Edgcumbe* on static display and 7029 *Clun Castle* in steam, March 2020. (Peter Zabek/GW Society)

APPENDIX

Weight diagram

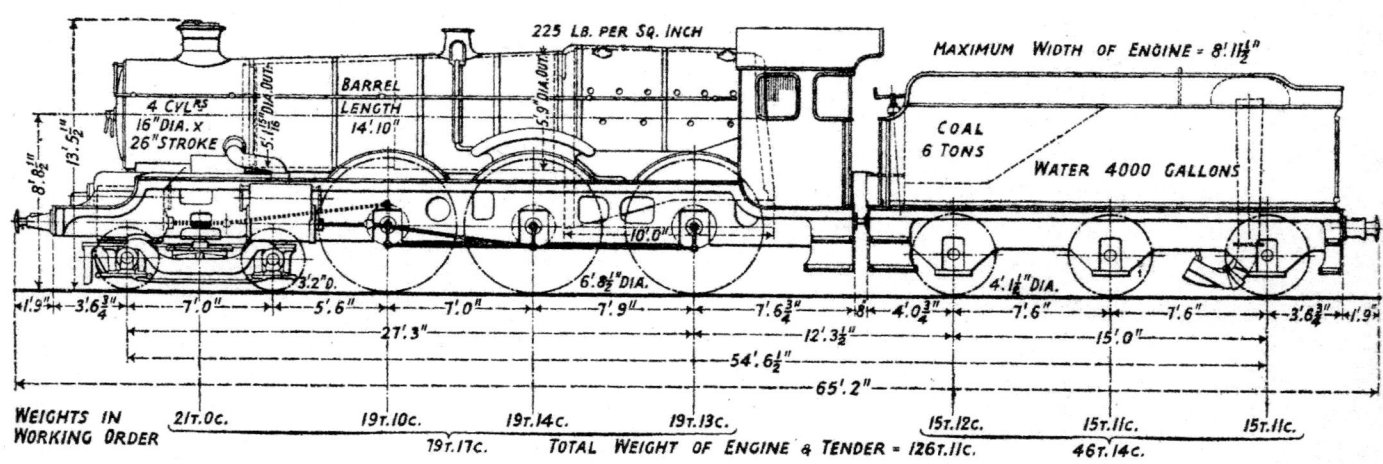

Statistics of the preserved Castles

No.	Built	Name	Double chimney	Withdrawn	Mileage
4073	8/23	*Caerphilly Castle*		5/60	1,910,730
4079	3/24	*Pendennis Castle*		5/64	1,758,398
5029	5/34	*Nunney Castle*		12/63	1,523,415
5043	3/36	*Barbury Castle*	5/58	12/63	1,400,817
	9/37	*Earl of Mount Edgcumbe*			
5051	5/36	*Drysllwyn Castle*		5/63	1,316,659
	8/37	*Earl Bathurst*			
5080	5/39	*Ogmore Castle*		4/63	1,117,030
	1/41	*Defiant*			
7027	9/49	*Thornbury Castle*		8/63	728,843
7029	5/50	*Clun Castle*	10/59	12/65	618,073 Mileage to 12/63 only

Allocations

4073:	8/23	Old Oak Common	4079:	3/24	Old Oak Common
	3/34	Cardiff Canton		5/25	Wembley Exhibition
	10/34	Landore		6/26	Old Oak Common
	4/35	Old Oak Common		9/31	Bristol Bath Road
	7/50	Bristol Bath Road		12/32	Stafford Road
	1/57	Cardiff Canton		12/35	Cardiff Canton
				11/39	Gloucester
				6/44	Hereford
5029:	5/34	Old Oak Common		11/48	Gloucester
	3/58	Worcester		6/53	Stafford Road
	5/59	Laira		6/57	Bristol Bath Road
	12/62	Cardiff East Dock		1/61	Bristol St Philip's Marsh
				8/62	Swindon
5043:	3/36	Old Oak Common	5051:	5/36	Landore
	6/52	Carmarthen		6/61	Neath
	2/56	Old Oak Common		2/63	Llanelly
	4/62	Cardiff Canton			
	9/62	Cardiff East Dock			
5080:	5/39	Old Oak Common	7027:	11/49	Laira
	8/40	Cardiff Canton		11/51	Old Oak Common
	12/55	Landore		4/60	Worcester
	9/61	Llanelly			
7029:	5/50	Newton Abbot			
	7/62	Old Oak Common			
	10/64	Gloucester			

INDEX

Allocations, 162
History
    4073, 30
    4079, 36-38
    4079 in Australia, 42-45
    4079, repatriation from Australia, 54-55
    4079, restoration, 62-69
    5029, 70-71
    5043, 76-77
    5043, restoration, 78-85
    5051, 120-122
    5080, 132-133
    7027, 136, 139
    7029, 141-146
    7029, restoration, 146-149
Logs
    4079
        Birkenhead Flyer, 13-15
    5043
        Bristolian, 95-96
        Carlisle – Hellifield, 97-98
        Crewe – Carlisle – Carnforth, 91-94
        Plymouth – Bristol, 100
        Shakespeare Express, 91
    7029
        Appleby – Ais Gill, 19
        King's Cross – Leeds, 16-19
        Lancaster – Carlisle, 18
        Lickey & Midlands, 10-13
Performance
    4079, 10
    5029, 71
    5043, 98-100
    7029, 15

Photographs, Locations (Black & White)
    Appleby, 29
    Australia, 45-48, 50-51
    Barry (Woodham Bros), 71, 85
    Beeston, 27
    Bristol Temple Meads, 21
    Caerphilly Works, 31
    Cardiff Canton, 30
    Cardiff General, 76
    Cardiff Goods, 121
    Carlisle, 28-29
    Chester, 24
    Crewe North, 38
    Dauntsey, 39
    Didcot, 44, 60-61, 124-126
    Gresford, 24-25
    Hooton, 25
    Leeds Holbeck, 27
    Neath, 136
    Newark, 26
    Newlay & Horsforth, 28
    Nottingham, 21
    Paddington, 31-32, 133
    Ranelagh Bridge, 23
    Sapperton, 23
    Science Museum (en route), 33
    Shrewsbury, 40, 134
    Swindon, 22, 77, 128, 137
    Tyseley, 150
    Worcester, 40
Photographs, Locations (Colour)
    Andover, 102
    Australia, 49, 51-53, 55-58
    Banbury, 103, 119, 150
    Barry (Woodham Bros), 122
    Bath, 105

Birmingham Moor Street, 108
Blea Moor, 19
Bristol Temple Meads, 106-107
Box, 104
Cardiff Goods Shed, 134
Cardiff Canton, 135
Carlisle, 101
Carnforth, 41
Chester, 41
Crewe, 118, 140
Cutnall Green, 156
Dainton, 129
Dawlish, 111
Didcot, 60-61, 73, 126-127, 131, 137
Dorridge, 157
Droitwich, 155, 159
East Largin Viaduct, 74
Euston, 109
Exeter St David's, 130
Forth Bridge, 114
Gloucester, 118
Hatton, 128
Llandudno Junction, 72
Lydney, 123
Newport, 129
Norton Junction, 157
Paddington, 103, 107, 113, 138
Peak Railway, 140
Plymouth, 118
Portbury Dock, Bristol, 59
Ribblehead, 112
Royal Oak, 70
Salisbury, 102
Shap, 20, 101
Songar Grange Crossing, 154
Stafford, 110

STEAM Museum, Swindon, 34-35
Stirling, 115-116
Swindon Works, 38, 126, 151
Taunton, 72
Toddington, 130
Tyseley, 86-90, 117, 135, 139, 151-153, 160
Whitlocks End, 154
Wilmcote, 158
Photographs, Locomotives (Black & White)
   4073, 30-33
   4079, 23-24, 39-41, 44-48, 50-51, 61
   4080, 37
   5029, 71
   5043, 76-77, 85
   5051, 121, 126-129
   5051, restoration, 124-126
   5080, 133-134
   7027, 136-137
   7029, 21-22, 25-29, 150
Photographs, Locomotives (Colour)
   3822, 131
   4073, 34-35
   4079, 38, 49, 51-53, 55-60
   5029, 70, 72-75
   5043, 101-119, 160
   5043, restoration, 86-90
   5051, 72, 122-123, 126, 128-131
   5080, 134-135, 160
   5322, 131
   6024, 74
   6998, 131
   7027, 137-140
   7029, 19-20, 129-130, 150-151, 153-160
   7029, restoration, 151-153
   D7052, 123
Railtours,
   4079 & 7029, 1965/6, 9-19
Statistics, 161
Weight Diagram, 161